Bill encouraged me and he encouraged all of us to never relent or grow weary in sharing the good news of our Lord Jesus Christ.

From the Foreword by
PAT ROBERTSON

BILL BRIGHT'S
"THE JOY OF KNOWING GOD"
SERIES

the JOY of SHARING JESUS

DR. BILL BRIGHT

The Bible Teacher's Teacher

COOK COMMUNICATIONS MINISTRIES
Colorado Springs, Colorado   •   Paris, Ontario
KINGSWAY COMMUNICATIONS LTD
Eastbourne, England

Victor® is an imprint of
Cook Communications Ministries,
Colorado Springs, CO 80918
Cook Communications, Paris, Ontario
Kingsway Communications, Eastbourne, England

THE JOY OF SHARING JESUS
© 2005 by BILL BRIGHT

First Printing, 2005
Printed in the United States of America
1 2 3 4 5 6 7 8 9 10 Printing/Year 09 08 07 06 05

Cover Design: Brand Navigation, LLC

Much of the text of this book is adapted by permission from
Witnessing Without Fear by Bill Bright (Thomas Nelson, 1992).

Library of Congress Cataloging-in-Publication Data

Bright, Bill.
 The joy of sharing Jesus : you have a story to tell / Bill Bright.
    p. cm. -- (The joy of knowing God series ; bk. 10)
 ISBN 0-7814-4255-9 (pbk.)
 1. Witness bearing (Christianity) I. Title. II. Series.

 BV4520.B648 2005
 248'.5--dc22

                                                          2004027062

Dedication

GLOBAL FOUNDING PARTNERS

The Bright Media Foundation continues the multifaceted ministries of Bill and Vonette Bright for generations yet unborn. God has touched and inspired the Brights through the ministries of writers through the centuries. Likewise, they wish to pass along God's message in Jesus Christ as they have experienced it, seeking to inspire, train, and transform lives, thereby helping to fulfill the Great Commission each year until our Lord returns.

Many generous friends have prayed and sacrificed to support the Bright Media Foundation's culturally relevant, creative works, in print and electronic forms. The following persons specifically have helped to establish the foundation. These special friends will always be known as Global Founding Partners *of the Bright Media Foundation.*

Bill and Christie Heavener and family

Stuart and Debra Sue Irby and family

Edward E. Haddock Jr., Edye Murphy-Haddock, and the Haddock family

Acknowledgments

It was my privilege to share fifty-four years, six months, and twenty days of married life with a man who loved Jesus passionately and served Him faithfully. Six months before his home going, Bill initiated what has become "The Joy of Knowing God" series. It was his desire to pass along to future generations the insights God had given him that they, too, could discover God's magnificence and live out the wonderful plan He has for their lives.

"The Joy of Knowing God" series is a collection of Bill Bright's top ten life-changing messages. Millions of people around the world have already benefited greatly from these spiritual truths and are now living the exciting Christian adventure that God desires for each of us.

On behalf of Bill, I want to thank the following team that helped research, compile, edit, and wordsmith the manuscripts and audio scripts in this series: Jim Bramlett, Rebecca Cotton, Eric Metaxas, Sheryl Moon, Cecil Price, Michael Richardson, Eric Stanford, and Rob Suggs.

I also want to thank Bill's longtime friends and Campus Crusade associates Bailey Marks and Ted Martin, who carefully reviewed the scripts and manuscripts for accuracy.

Bill was deeply grateful to Bob Angelotti and Don Stillman of Allegiant Marketing Group for their encouragement to produce this series and their ingenuity in facilitating distribution to so many.

A special thanks to Cook Communications and its team of dedicated professionals who partnered with Bright Media Foundation in this venture, as well as to Steve Laube, who brought us together.

Last but not least, I want to express my appreciation to Helmut Teichert, who worked faithfully and diligently in overseeing this team that Bill's vision would be realized, and to John Nill, CEO of Bright Media, who has helped me navigate the many challenges along this journey.

As a result of the hard work of so many, and especially our wonderful Lord's promise of His grace, I trust that multitudes worldwide will experience a greater joy by knowing God and His ways more fully.

With a grateful heart,
MRS. BILL BRIGHT (VONETTE)

Contents

Foreword

The Bible says that God gave Solomon largeness of heart. God gave Bill Bright largeness of heart.

Bill's heart was large with the love of Jesus, so much so that sharing God's great love with others came so natural for him. It just bubbled up from his innermost being. He could not stand the thought of passing up an opportunity to tell someone about our Savior, who died for all, that we might live. Bill wanted everyone on earth to hear this good news, and he spent his life at this task.

As one who also leads a ministry involved in world evangelization, I can honestly say that the ministry Bill founded, led, and inspired is probably the most significant of any that came into being in the twentieth century. I commend him as a great man of faith and a man who truly loved Jesus with all his heart.

Bill and I joined together in 1980 as co-program directors for Washington for Jesus, where five hundred thousand people gathered on the mall in Washington, D.C., and prayed from 6:00 a.m. to 5:00 p.m. They prayed for our nation, which was founded on the Bible and which God had raised up as the greatest missionary-sending nation in history, but which was turning against God. Bill and I were convinced that it was the prayers offered by those people that later opened many doors for evangelism and sharing the love of Jesus in the former Soviet Union and elsewhere.

Bill was a great patriot, but as always, his underlying motive was the fulfillment of the Great Commission. He was very concerned about our freedom in the United States to continue to share Christ with the liberty experienced in the past.

My life has been touched by Bill Bright, who was like the man in the Bible named Barnabas, the son of encouragement. Bill encouraged me and he encouraged all of us to never relent or grow weary in sharing the good news of our Lord Jesus Christ.

There was never a more faithful friend or greater servant of the Lord.

—PAT ROBERTSON

1

The Shy Overachiever

If you are a Christian but you tend to shrink from telling others about Jesus Christ, you're not alone!

Witnessing for our Lord is something most of us, in our hearts, know we should do. Yet we hesitate. To intrude in someone's life seems not only threatening but also presumptuous. We fear being offensive, fear being rejected, fear blundering what we'll say, and fear being considered fanatics.

So we remain silent—and hope that God will use someone else to get His message to those around us who do not know Him. Believe it or not, even though I founded a burgeoning worldwide evangelistic ministry, witnessing does not come naturally or easily to me either. By nature I'm a shy, reserved person, and initiating conversations with strangers is sometimes difficult for me. Even sharing the greatest news ever announced—that "God so loved the world that He gave His only begotten Son, that whoever believes in Him should not perish but have everlasting life" (John 3:16 NKJV)—is not always as easy for me as you might imagine.

So it might seem incongruous that God called a shy young

man almost sixty years ago to launch an evangelistic ministry that would become Campus Crusade for Christ International. Telling nonbelievers about Jesus, and training Christian laypeople to do so, is our primary calling. But I still can't say that evangelism is my spiritual gift.

What I do know is that God has made it crystal clear in His Word that every Christian is to "go and make disciples of all the nations" (Matthew 28:19). I've tried to be obedient to this command, and God has honored my obedience. He has transformed my personal witness from one of shy hesitancy to one of confident initiative. And He can do so for you, too!

If you'll pay attention to the principles in this book, you will find that you need never again be afraid of being embarrassed in a witnessing situation. These principles will give you the essential Scriptures and key thoughts to share with an interested listener, and by applying them you will find it more and more natural to begin a conversation about Jesus and guide a friend to a trusting relationship with Him.

> *You may be thinking, "This may work for someone else, but not for me."*

FROM COMPLACENCY TO CONFIDENCE

At this point you may be thinking, *This may work for someone else, but not for me.* Not so fast! We have seen thousands of Christians who were, at first, totally convinced that learning to share Jesus with others was not for them. It was too simple, they were too shy, or we "didn't know *their* situation." But they emerged from the training you're going to receive in this little book with their spirits rejoicing that God had transformed their witness, too—from complacency or shyness to confident initiative. Believe me, God will do the same for you.

As you read *The Joy of Sharing Jesus: You Have a Story to Tell*, ask God to show you how to apply these principles in your own life. Practice them with a Christian friend, then begin to apply what you are learning on a regular basis. I'm confident you will be excited with the results. Soon, in spite of any failures or hesitancies of the past, you will be a much more effective witness for our Lord.

> *I grew up thinking that Christianity was for women and children.*

But before we go there, I think it will encourage you to hear of my personal journey in learning to share Jesus with others.

AMBITIOUS OVERACHIEVER … AND STILL SHY

Why don't you come to church with us?" my landlords asked me practically every time I saw them.

For many weeks I would smile and thank this nice elderly couple for the invitation and then come up with an excuse. I had seldom attended church since I left home for college, and I preferred to spend my Sundays doing an amateur radio broadcast and going horseback riding in the Hollywood Hills.

I had gone into business in Hollywood, California, in the 1940s. And this godly couple, who must have been in their eighties, were reaching out to me in probably the only way they knew.

They didn't know that their efforts would one day result in my receiving Christ.

As I grew up in Coweta, Oklahoma, my mother had been a

dedicated Christian, but my father had not. So, in what I thought was the macho image of my father and grandfather, I grew up thinking that Christianity was for women and children, not for men. I was determined that, in spite of my shy nature, I would become strong and self-reliant and would accomplish anything I set out to accomplish.

Thus in college I worked hard to become student body president, editor of the college yearbook, named to *Who's Who in American Colleges and Universities*, and graduate as the "Outstanding Student." I was an agnostic, not knowing if God existed and not really caring whether He did. I believed that "a man can do anything he wants to, on his own." My father and grandfather had modeled that philosophy for me, and I had proven it to myself.

As a very materialistic young man seeking to prove myself, I wanted more.

But my ambitions didn't stop upon graduation. After college I was appointed to the faculty of Oklahoma State University. Since I had been reared on a ranch, I was assigned to serve as a member of the extension department, where I consulted with farmers and ranchers on various agricultural and cattle projects. I was paid many times what I was worth, but it wasn't enough. As a very materialistic young man seeking to prove myself, I wanted more.

There were several career options open to me, but the most attractive was a move to Los Angeles where, through a series of events, I ended up in business for myself in Hollywood. That's where I met the charming elderly couple who became my landlords.

"Why don't you come to church with us?" they continued to ask me. We lived right down the street from Hollywood

Presbyterian Church, and this loving white-haired couple seemed to take delight in attending the services.

"We have a great preacher by the name of Louie Evans," they persisted. "You'd love Dr. Evans."

Well, I couldn't imagine loving any preacher, but God was using this couple, along with my mother's prayers, to sow a seed in my heart. One Sunday evening I returned from an afternoon of horseback riding, smelling like a horse myself, and I decided to drop in on the evening service. I arrived after the program started, sat by myself in the back row, and left before the service was over so no one would see me—or smell me.

So much for church.

Or so I thought.

A BELIEF BADLY SHAKEN

Apparently, my landlords had given my name to someone in the college department at the church. A few days later I received a call from a young woman with an appealing invitation: "Bill, we're having a big party at [she gave the name of a famous movie star's] ranch and would love to have you join us. How about it?"

I couldn't think of an excuse quickly enough, so I ended up going. And I was in for quite a surprise. Gathered together in a big play barn were three hundred of the sharpest college-age men and women I have ever seen. They were happy, they were having fun, and they obviously loved the Lord. In one evening, my notion that Christianity was a women-and-children-only proposition had been badly shaken. I had never met people like this before.

Although I was busy building my business (a fancy foods

enterprise called "Bright's California Confections"), I began attending the college group's meetings at the church, as well as the regular church services. My shyness prevented me from mixing very much, and I always sat in the back row. But I listened to what they were saying, and eventually I fished out a long-unused Bible from a box of books and began to read and study on my own.

There were a number of successful businessmen in the church, including a prominent builder who would invite small groups of young people to his home for picnics and a swim in his pool. During one of those popular events, we asked him about his business and what it was like to be so successful.

His answer startled me. "Material success is not where you find happiness," he stated firmly. "There are rich people all over this city who are the most miserable people you'll ever meet. Knowing and serving Jesus Christ is what's important. He is the only way to find happiness."

This same principle had been exemplified by my godly mother. But somehow she hadn't verbalized it in a way that caught my attention, to make me realize my need to receive Christ as my personal Savior and Lord. But she lived it—and now I was meeting dynamic college kids and successful men and women who were living what my mother had lived, and who had been taught how to verbalize their faith, too.

INTELLECTUAL INTEGRITY BECKONS

Over a period of months, I began to be greatly impressed with the eloquence and personality of Dr. Louis Evans. He presented Jesus Christ and the Christian life in an attractive way I had never known before. So, as a matter of intellectual integrity, I was forced to begin an in-depth study of the life of Jesus—and the more I read and studied, the more I became convinced that He was more than just a great historical figure. He was truly the Son of God.

One Sunday in 1945, Dr. Henrietta C. Mears, director of Christian education at the church, spoke to our college and young-adult group about Paul's conversion experience on the road to Damascus. I had read the account before, but Dr. Mears made it come alive that evening

"Who are You, Lord, and what will You have me do?"

as she told of this ambitious man who was committed to ridding the world of the new heresy called Christianity. She told how Paul (then Saul) had been blinded by a bright light. Saul then asked, "Who are You, Lord ... and what will You have me do?"

"This is one of the most important questions you can possibly ask of God—even today," Dr. Mears told us. "The happiest people in the world are those who are in the center of God's will. The most miserable are those who are not doing God's will.

"Paul deceived himself into thinking he was doing God's will by persecuting the Christians. In reality, he was pursuing his own ambitions. So God set him straight through this dramatic experience on the road to Damascus."

As Dr. Mears spoke, I couldn't help noticing her wisdom, her boldness, and her love. She was another proof that my stereotype of Christianity had been all wrong. She spoke with authority, yet I could tell she held a genuine love for each of the young men and women in the audience.

"Now, not many of us have dramatic, emotional conversion

experiences as Paul did," she continued. "But the circumstances don't really matter. What matters is your response to
that same question: 'Who are You, Lord, and what will You
have me do?'"

She challenged each of us to go home, get on our knees,
and ask God that all-important question.

"WHAT WILL YOU HAVE ME DO?"

As I returned to my apartment that night, I realized that I
was ready to give my life to God. I was not really aware of
being lost, because I lived a relatively moral, ethical life. I
didn't feel that I had an unfilled need. (I was indeed lost and
in need but was not aware of it at the time.) What attracted me
most was God's love, which had been made known to me
through my study of the Bible and through the lives of the
people I had met at Hollywood Presbyterian Church.

I knelt beside my bed that night and asked the question
with which Dr. Mears had challenged us: "Who are You, Lord,
and what will You have me do?" In a sense, that was my prayer

*Nothing dramatic or
emotional happened
when I prayed.*

for salvation. It wasn't very profound
theologically, but the Lord knew my
heart, and He interpreted what was
going on inside me. Through my
study I now believed Jesus Christ was
the Son of God, that He had died for
my sin, and that, as Dr. Mears had shared with us, if I invited
Him into my life as Savior and Lord, He would come in
(Revelation 3:20).

Though nothing dramatic or emotional happened when I
prayed, I know without a doubt that Jesus did come into my
life, just as He promised He would. Asking Him that question

didn't seem very dynamic at first, but as I began to grow in my new commitment and love for the Lord, I became more and more aware of what a sinner I am and what a wonderful, forgiving Savior He is.

In time, I was elected president of the Sunday school class and met regularly with Dr. Mears and the other class officers to pray together and discuss the profound truths of God's Word. And although I didn't realize it at the time, God was cultivating within me a desire to share with others the new life I had discovered in Christ.

But He never did take away my shyness.

---❖---

"Go into all the world and preach the Good News to everyone, everywhere. Anyone who believes and is baptized will be saved. But anyone who refuses to believe will be condemned."

—Jesus Christ

2

Telling My Father about Jesus

Perhaps shyness is my "thorn in the flesh" because, as several friends have told me, people often expect the founder and president of a large, international evangelistic ministry to be specially gifted by God to be outgoing, gregarious, and a natural conversationalist. How wrong they would be!

Perhaps God knew that if He made witnessing easy for me, I might get the idea that it was me, and not Him, doing the work of transformation in people's hearts. This way, I have to be dependent on Him, which is exactly where He wants all of us whether we're shy or not.

I sure had to depend on Him the first time I shared Jesus, because I was scared to death. It was late 1945, and I remember it as though it happened just this morning. (I guess when your adrenalin is pumping and your heart is in your throat, you remember things more clearly.)

Bob was an outstanding young businessman who had just begun attending our church. As I became acquainted with him, I felt that the Lord wanted me to talk with Bob about his salvation … but I had no idea what to say.

Maybe I can get Dr. Evans or Dr. Mears to talk with him, I rationalized. *They're good at this kind of thing.*

But I couldn't shake the uncomfortable feeling that for some reason, God wanted me—not Dr. Evans or Dr. Mears—

─────────❖─────────

I felt that the Lord wanted me to talk with Bob, but I had no idea what to say.

─────────────────

to be the one. *But he's a sharp guy,* I argued, *and he'll raise questions I can't answer. Or he'll say no and I'll be embarrassed.*

It's amazing, isn't it, how logical we can sound when trying to justify our disobedience?

These sounded like good arguments at the time. But something kept reminding me of Matthew 4:19: "Follow Me, and I will make you fishers of men" (NKJV). I realized it was my responsibility to simply follow the Lord and obey Him. His responsibility is to do the inner work of changing human hearts.

ARGUING WITH THE HOLY SPIRIT

God also brought to mind Mark 16:15–16: "Go into all the world and preach the Good News to everyone, everywhere. Anyone who believes and is baptized will be saved. But anyone who refuses to believe will be condemned." The more I rationalized and the more I argued, the more the Holy Spirit seemed to tell me that Christ's command is just that—a command. It is not optional. If we love Him, we obey Him.

So, with mouth dry and heart pounding, I decided to tell Bob my personal story. As we sat in his car, half a block from the front of the church, I simply told him what you have just read. I showed Bob some Scriptures highlighting man's need for God, how to receive Christ as one's Savior and Lord, and shared how I had taken that pivotal step in my life. To my amazement and delight, Bob was as ready as anyone could be. When I invited him to join me in a prayer of personal commitment, he prayed right there, asking the Lord Jesus to forgive him of his sin and to come into his life.

God had special plans for Bob. Shortly after he became a Christian, Bob resigned his business position and entered seminary. He has been a minister for many years now, helping thousands of others to trust Christ and grow in their walk with Him.

TELLING MY FATHER

That first experience encouraged me to begin praying regularly for my father. Dad had never gone to church. He loved and respected my mother, who went to church regularly and took the children with her, but he wouldn't have anything to do with the church.

I loved Dad and wanted him to realize what he was missing. So in the spring of 1946, I drove all the way back to Oklahoma to talk to him.

"Dad, I've discovered something that has really changed my life," I began, "and I'd like to tell you about it. Would that be all right?"

I could tell he was curious, although cautious. "Why, sure … I suppose so," he responded.

As we sat in the living room, I felt nervous. *What is he thinking deep inside? Will he resent his upstart son being forward with him?*

I had been praying for my father for months, and now I

breathed another quick prayer for help. *Lord, there's no turning back now! Help me present You to my dad accurately and with confidence. And help Dad to be open to Your leading.*

"You know, Dad, how I've always believed that Mother's religion was all right for her but not for me?" I began. "How church was good for our basic moral values but nothing to get real personal about?"

Dad agreed, still cautious of what I might be leading to. "We both worked very hard to bring all of you up right," he said.

"And you did bring us up right," I assured him. "I appreciate that so much."

"Dad, I've discovered that it's possible to know God personally."

We chatted a while about my growing-up years and laughed at some of the awkward times. There was a warm, reflective smile on Dad's face as we spoke.

Then we talked about my business in California and the friends I had made in the church there. "Dad, I've discovered that it's possible to know God personally," I ventured. "I began to study what the Bible says about man's relationship with God. It says that 'God so loved the world, that He gave His only begotten Son, that whoever believes in Him should not perish, but have eternal life.' But it also says, 'All have sinned, and come short of the glory of God.'"

"I'm familiar with those things." He squirmed just a bit in his overstuffed chair. "I've heard them before."

"So had I," I agreed. "But I had never related those verses to my life. As I studied them, and other parts of the Bible, I began to realize how much God loves me—and you. He sent His Son Jesus to die on the cross for our sins."

"I've always lived a good, clean life," Dad said. His eyes looked over my shoulder at the drapes, then over at the book-shelves, then at the floor—but not at me. "I've never cheated anyone in my life."

A SMOKE SCREEN

My father had just brought up what I have since learned is a common smoke screen: *I'm good and moral … isn't that enough to get me to heaven?* I wanted to be very careful that I didn't come across as ungrateful or unloving. In fact, I loved Dad so much that it was all I could do to keep from preaching salvation to him camp-meeting style! But I knew that, as with most family members and close friends, loving gentleness was the approach to take with my father.

"Dad, I found out that it comes down to a personal deci-sion—a commitment of faith in Jesus Christ."

I picked up my Bible from a nearby end table and moved to the footstool beside him, turning to Ephesians 2:8–9.

"The Bible says, 'For by grace you have been saved through faith, and that not of yourselves; it is the gift of God, not of works, lest anyone should boast.' Most people think just like you, Dad—that living a good life is all that's necessary to get us to heaven. But God's Word says we've all fallen short of His standard. It's only through His grace that we can be saved, if we accept Him."

"What does it mean by *accept Him?*"

I turned to Revelation 3:20. "Jesus Christ himself said, 'Behold, I stand at the door and knock. If anyone hears My voice and opens the door, I will come in to him …' So it's simply a matter of inviting Jesus Christ into your life. That's what I've done, Dad, and I can't describe to you the deep-down joy and peace I've experienced since then. I've really felt God's love. And He has that same kind of love for you."

Dad studied his shoes, then worked at an imaginary loose thread near the knee of his trousers. He seemed much more open to the gospel than I had thought he would be. My excitement grew.

I felt sure he was going to pray with me right there, just as Bob had done in the car back in Hollywood. I decided I had said enough, that the next words should be Dad's. So I waited, watching him, trying to stay calm, and praying silently as he thought.

After several moments, he opened his mouth to speak.

I leaned forward expectantly.

"I need to know more, and I need to think about it," he sighed. "But I want to thank you, Son, for talking to me."

My father did not receive Christ during that visit to Oklahoma.

ANOTHER CHANCE

Though disappointed that my father had not given his life to Jesus, I was somewhat encouraged that he had been open to the gospel message. I continued praying for Dad through that spring and summer, and since I had arranged to attend Princeton Seminary that fall, I wrote home that I would be in Coweta for a three-day stopover en route to Princeton, New Jersey.

My mother wrote back that during that same week, the tiny Methodist church in town would be holding a series of revival services.

Could this be the time my dad would give his life to Christ? I had a strong feeling—as if the Lord was assuring me—that this revival campaign just might be God's special timing. As I drove nonstop from California, I could feel the excitement building inside me. The service started at 7:00 p.m., and I arrived home at 6:00.

"Are you going to the church service?" I asked Mother and Dad, after I had greeted them.

God knew that I still had the tendency to let cowardice get the best of me.

"We hadn't planned on it," Dad replied.

"Would you go with Vonette and me?" I had recently become engaged to Vonette Zachary, who had also been raised in the community. Of course, Mother wanted to go. She looked at Dad.

"Sure, we'll go with you," he said.

The revival preacher was an old-fashioned evangelist: He put lots of energy into his sermons, called sin sin and the Devil the Devil, and after every message he urged sinners to the front of the church to give their lives to Jesus. But in Coweta he had been preaching for more than a week with no response. Not one person had come forward to repent of sin and receive Christ as Savior and Lord.

And this night was no different. "I feel God moving here tonight," he implored, "and if you aren't saved, God is telling you to come down here and turn your life over to Him. Now while we sing this next verse, come to the altar and give your life to Jesus Christ."

As we sang, I prayed for my father. I had left Mother and Dad at the church and rushed to pick up Vonette, and by the time we arrived, the church was full. We had found two seats on the side of the sanctuary opposite my parents. Now, as we sang the hymn, I watched out of the corner of my eye.

End of the first verse. No one had moved.

The preacher spoke again, perspiration glistening from his brow: "Do you have a loved one who is here and not a believer, and you've been praying for him? Get out of your seat and go put your arm around him and bring him to the altar."

I have never been one who likes to use pressure or coercion of any kind, especially when it comes to spiritual commitments. And at first I cringed at what the preacher suggested. Within just a few moments, however, I sensed the Lord nudging me to go talk with Dad.

But, Lord, I pleaded, *the Bright family is well known in this community, and Dad has a lot of pride. This is going to embarrass him. Do You really want me to do it?*

> *Dad's idea of a Christian conversion was stereotypical: a lightning bolt from the sky or a blinding light.*

God knew that I still had the tendency to let cowardice get the best of me, for before I could argue further, I found myself out of my seat and walking all the way across the church toward Dad.

I put my arm around him. "Dad," I whispered, "come with me to the altar."

He did, and Mother joined us.

I didn't know then what I know now about leading a person to Jesus Christ. So Dad and I both knelt at the altar and wept while the preacher led the audience in another verse of the hymn. Dad cried and I cried, and I urged him to ask Jesus into his heart, but he didn't. Jesus was knocking at the door, but Dad didn't know how to open it.

No one else had responded to the invitation, so the service ended. I took Vonette to her home, then rushed home to talk to Dad.

LOOKING FOR LIGHTNING

He didn't talk much, and I knew better than to press him. But something from our brief words that evening stands out to me today, even though I didn't recognize it then: *Dad had been looking for an emotional experience.* His idea of a Christian conversion was stereotypical: a lightning bolt from the sky or a blinding light, like that experienced by the apostle Paul. Since that type of thing hadn't happened at the altar, Dad felt that he hadn't "broken through."

The next night, it happened all over again. A rousing sermon. An altar call. The preacher urging us to "put your arm around a loved one and bring him to the altar." And my dad and me walking to the altar, with Mother alongside us, and kneeling and weeping at the front of that church.

As we knelt, Vonette joined us. And this time, my father invited Jesus Christ into his life wholeheartedly, unreservedly. I saw a visible change in his eyes, from complacency to joy. Then he thanked God for entering his life and beginning the change process.

But Dad wasn't done yet. He got off his knees and went back to where he had been sitting. He put his arm around a young man and invited him to join us at the altar.

That young man was my brother, who had just returned from the war in Europe. (He did not come forward that night, but years afterward he assured me that he had later received Christ into his life.)

My father was a changed man after that night, and he lived

thirty-six more years as a child of God before he went to heaven at age ninety-three. Eventually, my entire family came to Christ.

LOVE, OBEDIENCE, AND INITIATIVE

Whenever I look back on how God brought me into His kingdom and began even then to show me how hungry people are to know Him, a key thought stands out to me. *All it took to begin my move toward God was the love and initiative of a few caring people:*

- My mother, who prayed for me every day.
- One elderly couple who loved the Lord and their church. They probably didn't know how to witness, but they personified love to me and invited me to their church.
- A group of caring, fun-loving Christian men and women who invited me to a barn party and welcomed me with open arms.
- A dynamic older woman by the name of Henrietta C. Mears, whose love for me and whose knowledge of the Scriptures made me want to know God's Word too.
- Several Christian businessmen, who believed in hard, honest work for an honest profit and exemplified the truth that real success comes only in knowing Jesus Christ.
- Dr. Louie Evans, then-pastor of Hollywood Presbyterian Church, whose consistent lifestyle and intelligent teaching and preaching of the Scriptures attracted me to the person of Jesus Christ.

As I think of these people and their influence on me, I realize that God has indeed called each of us to personify Jesus Christ to the people with whom we come in contact every day.

Loving others, showing them Jesus Christ in word and deed, is not a job just for pastors or ministry workers. It's a joyful task to which God has commissioned everyone who calls himself Christian.

To whom is God leading you today, to demonstrate His love and to tell your story?

Chances are you'll be just as nervous as I was when you begin to share your faith. But my early experiences showed me that you don't have to wait until you feel "expert enough." It surely wasn't my expertise that led Bob and my father and eventually other members of my family to Jesus—it was simply the fact that I wanted to obey God, who prompted me to share my faith with them. I was so awkward at first, but God worked through me and in spite of me.

The keys were love, obedience, and initiative. Despite my faltering shyness, God spoke to these people. You can have the same confidence that, if you reach out in genuine love, He will use you—no matter how nervous you may feel.

"I AM THE WAY, AND THE TRUTH, AND THE LIFE; NO ONE COMES TO THE FATHER BUT THROUGH ME."

—JESUS CHRIST

3

Why Sharing Jesus Makes Sense

Have you ever felt hesitant to share the good news of Jesus Christ because you thought the other person would not be interested, might respond with hostility, or would consider you "one of those fanatics"?

Or have you been slow to share your faith because you didn't feel you have the gift of evangelism, and witnessing is better left to those with the "gift"?

These are emotions every Christian has felt at one time or another. I certainly have struggled with them. However, during many years of sharing Jesus and training others to do the same, I have been unable to find any biblical rationale to justify those reasons for not telling others about Him. In fact, from my study of God's Word as well as from my personal experience, I can identify five key reasons that compel *every* Christian to share Jesus with others.

THE CLEAR COMMAND

Jesus Christ's last command to the Christian community was, "Go into all the world and preach the Good News to everyone, everywhere" (Mark 16:15). This command, which the church calls the Great Commission, was not intended merely for the disciples or for the apostles or for those Christians who may have the gift of evangelism. Heeding Jesus' command is the duty of every man and woman who confesses Christ as Lord. We cannot pick and choose which commands of our Lord we will follow.

WHEN YOU CARE, YOU SHARE

Jesus said, "I am the way, and the truth, and the life; no one comes to the Father but through Me" (John 14:6 NASB). Men and women are truly lost without Him. According to God's Word, Jesus Christ is the only way to bridge the gap between man and God. Without Him, people cannot know God and have no hope of eternal life.

As children of God, we care deeply about others who do not yet know Him, others who do not know with confidence that they're en route to heaven once their earthly life is through. We care that they discover new life in Christ, who is the spiritual solution to their every need now and forever.

When you care, you share.

THE "GOD-SHAPED VACUUM"

Today more than ever, people around us are seeking a spiritual solution to their problems or a greater sense of spiritual centeredness. French physicist and philosopher Blaise Pascal called this spiritual void the "God-shaped vacuum." How to fill it? His answer is timeless: "[It] cannot be satisfied by any created thing," Pascal continued, "but only by God, the Creator, made known through Jesus Christ."

People have always sought a spiritual answer and new life.

You and I have found the answer; we've found new life. So why not share the joy? Those around you are more interested in your story than you may think.

Shortly after Vonette and I began working with college students on the UCLA campus, we were scheduled to speak at the Kappa Alpha Theta sorority. The sorority was nicknamed "the house of beautiful women," and indeed they were. Sixty of them gathered in the living room to hear us speak.

> *The sorority was nick-named "the house of beautiful women," and indeed they were.*

At that time, the student newspaper and student government were controlled by the radical Left due to active communist-recruitment activity on campus. I must confess to you that, as I prepared for this event, it occurred to me (more than once) that my audience would have little interest in what I planned to say. I prayed that God would break through this atmosphere and reach at least one or two of the young women.

When I finished my message, I said, "If you would like to know Jesus Christ personally, come and tell me." I had prayed that one or two would come. But at least thirty of these beautiful college women stood in line to tell me they wanted to become Christians.

Why was I surprised? Because I had doubted that they would be interested in my message. I had discounted the fact that nearly everyone, everywhere, seeks spiritual truth to fill that God-shaped vacuum.

Since this was my first group meeting in which people wanted to receive Christ, I didn't know what to do next. So I did what any good businessman does when he's not sure what to do: I called another meeting. "Vonette and I would like to invite all of you to our home tomorrow night," I announced. "We'll talk more about how you can know Christ personally. Will you come?"

Each of the women agreed, and most of them came—some with their boyfriends. All but a few trusted Christ that evening. It was from this nucleus that our ministry spread not only across the UCLA campus, but also eventually across the country and around the globe.

These sharp young women and their boyfriends had been seeking spiritual answers. They had been hungry for the good news. They were waiting only for someone to tell them, someone to show them how.

Why was I surprised? Because I had doubted that they would be interested in my message.

I believe that the best way to approach sharing Jesus with others is to always assume that the family member, neighbor, coworker, or person you've just met will be interested in the good news you have to tell. They're seeking a spiritual answer—and Jesus *is* the answer!

THE BEST NEWS EVER!

We Christians have in our possession the greatest gift available to humankind—the greatest news ever announced. Christ is risen! We serve a living Savior, who not only lives within us in all His resurrection power but also has assured us of eternal life. He died on the cross in our place for our sin, then rose from the dead. We have direct fellowship with God through Jesus Christ. And this fellowship, this peace, this gift of eternal life, is available to all who receive Him.

Why are we so hesitant to share this good news? Why is it that we so readily discuss our political views or athletic preferences, our gas mileage or utility bills, our children's growing pains or our office gossip, but clam up when it comes to discussing the greatest news ever announced?

> *Our faith should be the number-one message on our lips.*

If our faith in Christ really means as much to us as it should, then it only follows that our faith should be the number-one message on our lips.

COMPELLED BY LOVE

The love of Jesus Christ for us, and our love for Him, compels us to tell others about Him. Helping to fulfill Christ's Great Commission is both a duty and a privilege. We share because we love Christ. We share because He loves us. We tell others because we want to honor and obey Him. We tell them because He gives us a special quality of love for them.

Whenever you're alone with someone, I encourage you to always consider it a divine appointment. Perhaps God brought this person across your path, at this very moment in time, in order for you to share the story you have to tell. You've experienced the good news, and this person needs to hear it.

Seize the day!

WALK BY THE SPIRIT, AND YOU WILL NOT
CARRY OUT THE DESIRE OF THE FLESH.

Galatians 5:16 NASB

4

Why Some Christians Hesitate

I don't wear my religion on my sleeve. My religion is personal and private, and I don't want to talk about it."

He was one of America's great statesmen—a Christian—and I had just briefed him on our organization's plan for world evangelism. As we talked about involving a thousand key Christian leaders in the effort, his statement startled me.

"You're a Christian, aren't you?" I asked him.

"Yes, I am," he replied, "but I'm not a religious fanatic."

I've heard this logic several times, and it grieves me every time I hear it. It grieved me that day as I heard this fine gentleman rationalize a passive faith.

I prodded gently: "Did it ever occur to you that it cost Jesus Christ His life so that you could say you're a Christian?"

He thought a moment but didn't respond.

"And it cost the disciples their lives," I continued. "Millions of Christians throughout the centuries have suffered and many have died as martyrs to get the message of God's love and forgiveness to you. Now do you really believe that your faith in Christ is something you shouldn't talk about?"

"No, sir," the man sighed. "I'm wrong. Tell me what I can do about it."

Without even realizing it, this gentleman had fallen for one of Satan's favorite lines: *One's faith should be a very private thing, something a person just doesn't talk about.* As a result, his witness for Christ was next to nil. He held in his possession the greatest news ever announced, but up to that point he had refused to share it.

❁

As a ministry that specializes in helping train laypeople in effective evangelism, we have made extensive studies of why Christians don't share their faith more readily. We've found that, while some believe that "religion should be personal and private," most Christians do recognize the biblical imperative for a personal witness. But they allow four barriers to keep them from witnessing without fear.

> *Ask God to reveal to you any areas of your life that are not right.*

SPIRITUAL LETHARGY

If you aren't excited about something, chances are you won't tell many people about it. And we find that in the lives of far too many Christians, the excitement of the Christian walk has been dulled by everyday distractions, materialistic pursuits, and unconfessed sin. In biblical terms, they have "lost their first love" for Jesus.

If you have felt spiritually dry or defeated, it is possible that you have drifted away from total devotion and obedience to Jesus Christ. Perhaps you've allowed the hectic pace of life to distract you from quality times of prayer and meditation in

God's Word. Perhaps you have allowed society's pervasive message of humanism and self-gratification to lure you toward "the good life"—and away from *the best life*. Perhaps these and other offenses toward God have festered into unconfessed sin.

If these symptoms of spiritual lethargy describe your state of heart, I want to assure you that you needn't continue to live that way! You can restore intimacy with the Savior by taking two important steps.

EXAMINE YOUR HEART FOR UNCONFESSED SIN

Wait quietly before God and ask Him to reveal to you any areas of your life that are not right. Is there a secret part of your life that you have not confessed to God? Do you need to ask forgiveness of someone? Of God?

To help you better understand the importance of confession, it is helpful to understand that the original meaning of the word *confess* means "to agree with." As you agree with God concerning sin in your life, you are saying at least three things to Him:

Have you fallen victim to some of the Enemy's "lines"?

- "God, I agree with You that these things I'm doing are wrong."
- "I agree with You that Christ died on the cross for these sins."
- "I repent—I consciously turn my mind and heart from my sins, and as a result I turn my actions toward obedience to You."

So as the Spirit brings unconfessed sin to mind, acknowledge and *agree with* God in prayer that you have sinned, and recommit to total obedience to God's plan for you.

I have often found it helpful to recite the liberating promise that I memorized years ago: "If we confess our sins, He is faithful and righteous to forgive us our sins and to cleanse us from all unrighteousness" (1 John 1:9 NASB). Praise God—He keeps His promises even when we do not! As we honestly confess our shortcomings to Him, He is faithful to forgive and wash away our unrighteousness.

Keeping "short accounts" with the heavenly Father in this way will help you overcome any spiritual lethargy that may hinder your witness for Him.

BE SURE YOU ARE CONTROLLED BY THE HOLY SPIRIT

The apostle Paul taught, "Walk by the Spirit, and you will not carry out the desire of the flesh" (Galatians 5:16 NASB). He's telling us that the secret to successful Christian living is to "walk by [or *in*] the Spirit," which simply means allowing God, through His Holy Spirit, to empower and guide us moment by moment, day by day.

Satan attempts to re-engineer innocent circumstances into distracting obstacles.

It is the Holy Spirit who will convict you when you've sinned, who will nudge you to extend a caring hand to a neighbor, who will give you a reservoir of love for others, who will urge you to share your faith with those around you. Obeying His quiet prompting will keep you from ever wanting to drift from your first love in Jesus Christ. (You will find much more about the Holy Spirit in *The Joy of Spirit-Filled Living* and other books in "The Joy of Knowing God" series.)

Don't let spiritual lethargy destroy God's plan for you to touch others with His love.

BELIEVING THE ENEMY'S "LINES"

Scripture is clear about it: There is a definite spiritual battle raging around us. "We wrestle not against flesh and blood, but against principalities, against powers, against the rulers of the darkness of this world" (Ephesians 6:12 KJV).

The Bible says that God "has rescued [Christians] from the one who rules in the kingdom of darkness" (Colossians 1:13). All of us were once members of that kingdom, and nonbelievers with whom we share Jesus are still members of Satan's kingdom. So count on it: Whenever you sense God leading you to tell someone about Jesus, Satan's agents will go to work on you. You may hear some very believable lines that are intended to make you think twice, turn heel, and abandon your good intentions. A small sampling will help prepare you to win the battle.

"YOU HAVE NO RIGHT TO FORCE YOUR VIEWS ON OTHERS"

You and I have heard this one a thousand times. And in today's relativistic culture, vocal anti-Christian forces even go so far as to label the good news of Jesus Christ "intolerant."

Whenever you hear this smoke screen, ask yourself, *Where would I be today if the person who introduced me to Christ had heeded this line?* When we share Christ in a spirit of gentle love, we aren't "forcing" our views on anyone. When we speak gently and lovingly, the hearer is free to listen, change the subject, or move away.

"YOU'RE GOING TO OFFEND HER"

If someone you know were dying of cancer and you knew the cure for the disease, would you avoid telling him about the cure for fear of offending him? Of course not. You would gladly share the good news that his cancer can be cured. Why should we be any less enthusiastic about sharing the ultimate cure over the ultimate disease?

"HE'LL THINK YOU'RE A FANATIC"

That's a popular one. And, yes, he might think you are a fanatic. But then again, he might be the one person God has specially prepared for you on this day. Not everyone will accept the gospel—even Jesus encountered men and women who rejected His message. Our role is not to convert but to obey. We can dislodge the "fanatic" or even the "intolerant" stereotype with a confident, loving, logical presentation of the claims of Christ, shared in the power of the Holy Spirit. The results are up to God, not us.

DISTRACTIONS AND INTERRUPTIONS

A phone rings. Someone else enters the room. The waiter stops by for the twelfth time to ask if everything's okay. A baby cries for attention. Someone turns on the television. When you set out to raid Satan's kingdom, you can count on one thing: He will do everything he can to reengineer innocent circumstances into distracting obstacles. The last thing the Enemy wants is for an open nonbeliever to learn of the love Christ has in store for him.

Our role is not to convert but to obey.

Whenever I find myself in such a situation, I'll pray silently, even as we're talking, that God would bind Satan and allow my friend to hear the message and make a free choice. Sharing Jesus is definitely a spiritual battle, but you can be assured that if Satan is causing problems, he's worried. And if he's worried, then you must be doing something right.

"HE'LL SAY NO AND YOU'LL BE EMBARRASSED"

We Christians are often guilty of presenting the gospel with a hesitancy that says, *Uh … you wouldn't want to receive the greatest gift available to mankind, would you?* We don't realize how many people are actually ready to receive Christ if only someone will show them how. Jesus assures us that

> *Jesus assures us that "the harvest is plentiful."*

"the harvest is plentiful" (Matthew 9:37 NASB). Thus we can always presuppose a positive response. Our philosophy of witnessing should not be, *I'm sure he'll say no to Jesus*, but rather, *Who could say no to Jesus?*

LACK OF PRACTICAL KNOW-HOW

Our surveys have shown us that, while the majority of Christians believe they *should* share their faith, many are hesitant because they don't know what to say. Later in this book we will address the essential "know-how" via a sample gospel presentation that has proved effective for thousands of Christians in a wide variety of real-life situations. I'm confident that you will find this training extremely helpful, so please stay with me.

FEAR OF FAILURE

There is one more key reason why some Christians hesitate to share Jesus with others, and it can so paralyze us that it warrants a chapter of its own:

Fear of failure.

Can you identify with that? I thought so.

So let's deal with it.

5

Conquering the Fear of Failure

I t hurts to be turned down. It can feel, well, downright *personal*. A rejection of our message feels like a rejection of our*selves*. None of us likes it.

And it's precisely for this reason that the fear of failure is one of the biggest cripplers of a faithful witness.

It hurts even more when we know we've reached out in genuine love only to see someone refuse the greatest gift ever offered to mankind: God's Son. Compassion for the lost does not come without tears. But one of the assuring facts of the Christian life is that God does not ask anything of us that His Son has not already gone through Himself.

Indeed, though Jesus attracted crowds from miles around, many rejected His message. Think on that for a moment: Not everyone who heard Jesus heeded Him. He was faithful in proclaiming salvation, yet many chose to despise and reject Him.

But who among us would consider Jesus' ministry a failure?

From His example, and from the ministry of millions of successful Christians through the centuries, we can draw a powerful conclusion regarding success or failure in witnessing: *When we obey and share Christ in an intelligent, loving way, we cannot fail!* The message might be accepted or rejected, but the results are not up to us. When you obey God and are motivated by love, you cannot fail. When you tell others your story in obedience to God's command and the Holy Spirit's leading, you succeed in witnessing, no matter what the imme-

God is responsible for heart-changes, not us.

diate result. God is responsible for heart-change, not us. We are simply the messengers He has chosen to convey the message.

This liberating concept can and should free up every Christian who may be paralyzed by the fear of failure. While we should be prepared to represent our Lord honorably, the results of our witness are in God's hands. Over the years our ministry has taught literally millions of fellow believers worldwide to share their faith with confidence, and we have so enjoyed watching these Christians breathe a huge sigh of relief when they comprehend this principle. We encourage them to memorize the following definition:

SUCCESSFUL WITNESSING

Success in witnessing is simply taking the initiative to share Christ in the power of the Holy Spirit and leaving the results to God.

SOME WILL DECLINE

For those who would question whether we should even try (considering the probability that a number of listeners will say no), we must remember the message Christ gave in the parable of the sower. You know the story … but please take time to review it again, carefully, right now:

> A farmer went out to plant some seed. As he scattered it across his field, some seeds fell on a footpath, and the birds came and ate them. Other seeds fell on shallow soil with underlying rock. The plants sprang up quickly, but they soon wilted beneath the hot sun and died because the roots had no nourishment in the shallow soil. Other seeds fell among thorns that shot up and choked out the tender blades. But some fell on fertile soil and produced a crop that was thirty, sixty, and even a hundred times as much as had been planted.

We just never know, really, where a "no" will lead.

> MATTHEW 13:3–8

There are four types of listeners (types of soil), Christ taught. And only one of four will take the message (the seed) and put it to work in his life.

The good ground represents the heart of a person who listens to the message and understands it and goes out and brings thirty, sixty, or even a hundred others into the kingdom (see Matthew 13:23).

The other three listeners will squander the message or reject it outright. Jesus himself recognized this, and though His compassion drove Him to love and long for every human soul, He knew that people would exercise their God-given power of free choice both for and against Him. And people continue to do so today.

So there will be noes. When they come, we should be neither surprised nor discouraged. Jesus experienced them and so will we.

And we just never know, really, where a no will lead.

NO WASTED WITNESS

I recall Tom and Dorrine, a married couple from Washington, D.C., who volunteered for a church neighborhood outreach campaign. They called on one home in which a man and woman lived together unmarried and, though friendly, were so high on drugs that they couldn't carry on a conversation.

Trust in God's timing.

So Tom and Dorrine left a gospel booklet on the coffee table and suggested that the couple read the booklet at a better time. Tom and Dorrine had received a no—unspoken yet unmistakable.

Two weeks later, and in a better state of mind, the woman came across the booklet and began to read. Its simple presentation convicted her, and she actually knelt in her living room and invited Christ into her life. She then gave the booklet to her boyfriend, and a few days later he read it and accepted the Lord.

As the weeks passed, this couple listened to Christian programs on radio and TV. One Sunday they visited the church down the block—the same church that had sent Tom and Dorrine out into the neighborhood.

When the pastor gave the invitation, the man and

woman went forward to declare their new faith in God and to be baptized. They ceased living together as singles, then soon were married. Five years later, they had grown so much in their walk with the Lord that he was asked to be a

PRAYER AND GOD'S TIMING

Just as Jesus prayed that the Holy Spirit would do a work in the lives of His disciples, so we can pray that the Holy Spirit will convict a nonbeliever and give him or her a strong desire for the ways of God.

God's Word assures us that God is "not willing that any should perish but that all should come to repentance" (2 Peter 3:9 NKJV). God desires the soul of your loved one, friend, or neighbor even more than you do.

Sometimes, however, in His mysterious and sovereign timing, He chooses to wait for the prayer of a concerned believer to unleash the Holy Spirit in that person's heart. As someone has said, "Prayer is not conquering God's reluctance but laying hold of God's willingness."

Neither wise words nor smooth techniques can draw a person to Christ. Only the Spirit of God can do so. By prayer, we seek His work in the lives of others. So pray in faith, believing that God will do the work you're asking Him to do.

Make a list of all for whom you're praying. Keep a prayer journal, and make notes of special things that happen to them as time passes. Ask God for the salvation of each friend and loved one, and realize the liberating truth that God loves them even more than you do. Pray regularly, thanking God in faith that He is at work, drawing them to himself. Trust in God's timing. Your friend or loved one may surprise you by eagerly accepting Christ upon first hearing the gospel. If the person does not respond at the first opportunity, continue to pray, thanking God in faith that He will answer according to His expressed will. Demonstrate unconditional love through continued fellowship with the person. Conscientiously model the positive, victorious Christian life through your attitudes, words, and actions.

As the Lord leads, talk about Jesus again in your conversations, without hesitancy or embarrassment. You have planted the seed. If it takes root in a fertile heart, God will harvest that seed in His sovereign timing. He may use you, He may use someone else, or He may bring your loved one to himself in a special way. So keep praying, loving, and trusting.

deacon in the church and she was active in several ministries.

Back when Tom and Dorrine left the haze of this couple's drug-filled living room, they must have thought, *What a waste of time!* But because of their initial contact, made in obedience to Jesus, who commanded, "Go, and preach the gospel," God turned this couple's no into a yes and brought two new believers into His kingdom.

There really is no wasted witness.

THE LETTER

A nother no that stands out in my memory is a long letter I wrote to a nationally known sales consultant. I had met him at a conference where he was the featured speaker.

We enjoyed a good conversation, and, as I told him what I do and shared my spiritual journey, he was noncommittal. "Why don't you drop me a line with some more information?" he said as we parted company.

Tom and Dorrine had received a no—unspoken yet unmistakable.

I thought and prayed about what I would write him. Over the next several days, I sensed the Lord's guidance as I pulled together key Scriptures and concepts explaining God's wonderful plan of redemption for mankind. I made a copy, mailed him the original, and prayed that God would use my effort in this man's life.

To this day, I do not know whether this gentleman ever accepted God's offer of new life through Jesus Christ.

He had given me an implied no.

But God was working in ways I never would have imagined.

As some trusted friends and I reviewed the letter I had written, they suggested that we print it in quantity, under a fictitious salutation, as a tool to help Christians explain the plan of salvation. We addressed the letter to a "Dr. Van Dusen" and printed several hundred copies. Millions of copies later, our staff and Christian laypeople worldwide continue to use this document to

I thought and prayed about what I would write him.

help nonbelievers understand and embrace God's plan. (See "The Letter," appendix A of this book.)

One evening several years later I received a long-distance phone call. The caller told me of a printed letter to a "Dr. Van Dusen" which she had found in the seat of a commercial airliner.

"Are you the Bill Bright who wrote this letter?" she asked. She proceeded to ask me some spiritual questions, which I answered as best I could. Suddenly she asked, "I would like to become a Christian. Can you help me?"

What a thrill it was to lead this sincere woman in prayer, over the phone, as she asked Christ into her life as Savior and Lord! But it didn't stop there. In her family room were five other adults—family and friends. Each of them had read her copy of the letter. One by one they came to the phone, and, after some questions and discussion, every one of them gave his or her heart and life to Jesus that evening.

It is unknown whether the original intended recipient of my letter ever responded as I had hoped. In the strictest sense, my attempt could be chalked up as a failure. But God doesn't do failure—He had results in store that were far beyond my wildest imagination.

There really is no wasted witness.

We fail in witnessing only when we fail to witness. When you take the initiative to share Christ in the power of the Holy Spirit and leave the results to God, there is no failure to fear.

6

Guiding a Conversation
toward Jesus

I had a great opportunity to talk with someone about Christ today," a bright young woman once told me, "but I just couldn't think of a way to begin. I felt very awkward. How do you guide a conversation toward Jesus, in a way that doesn't seem contrived?"

A common concern. Many Christians have confided to us that guiding a conversation toward Jesus is often the toughest portion of the sharing experience. At one extreme, some well-intended folks practically shout "Repent!" as if from a street corner in the inner city. At the other extreme, other folks inch their way *ever … so … cautiously* toward spiritual things—so cautiously, in fact, that the conversation never gets around to the Savior.

Personally, I'm uncomfortable with the first approach. And I know from experience that the second can get so easily side-tracked that the gospel loses out to the weather, football, or stories of Johnny's latest escapades at school. There needs to be a happy medium—a means of turning a conversation toward Christ that is natural and sensitive, yet that helps those we talk with realize the need for the Savior.

THE TRANSITION

One method we've found effective in transitioning a conversation to the gospel is a sequence of four directed questions. They can be used whether you have known someone just a few minutes or for a lifetime. The questions are especially helpful to use after a non-Christian has attended a Christian event (church service, lecture, concert, seminar) or if you have given the nonbeliever a Christian book, magazine, or audio message. Following the event, or after the person has had a chance to read or listen to what you gave him, pose the questions in the following order:

1. "What did you think of the (concert, message, book)?"
2. "Did it make sense to you?"
3. "Have you made the wonderful discovery of knowing Christ personally?"
4. "You'd like to, wouldn't you?" Or, "Would you like to?"

Listen intently to the person's answer to each question; then ask the next one in the sequence. You'll see that each subsequent question is appropriate to ask no matter what answer was given to the preceding question. The fourth question provides a natural lead-in to a discussion of the gospel.

But let me emphasize that without the proper motivation—love—these questions could sound like an inquisition. So it is vital that you be motivated by Christlike love and compassion and that you ask the questions gently, with a friendly expression on your face and a caring tone in your voice.

Also keep in mind that a common mistake among Christians who are beginning to share their faith is that they allow conversations to become sidetracked. It is generally best not to talk about religions, denominations, churches, and personalities. Many people have bitter remembrances—real or imagined—from their past about these peripheral issues. But if you stay focused on the person of Jesus Christ, your listener can't help but be attracted to Him.

A STORY TO TELL

If you have time, use stories. *You* have a story to tell! The word *witness* literally means to give testimony of facts or events. In other words, to witness is to tell the true story of how Christ has changed your life and the lives of others.

> *Guiding a conversation toward Jesus is often the toughest portion of the sharing experience.*

The New Testament Christians witnessed by telling stories of how Jesus Christ died and rose from the dead, how He changed their lives, and what He offered to everyone who would receive Him. Paul told of his dramatic conversion experience. Their witness through stories not only caught the attention of the listeners, but also showed them vividly how they, too, could commit themselves to the Lord.

At Campus Crusade for Christ we have each of our new staff, and everyone who goes through our training conferences, write and practice giving a three-minute testimony. A well-crafted personal testimony covers at least these three basic points:

- what your life was like before you received Christ,
- how you received Christ, and
- what your life is like since you received Christ.

We encourage everyone to be as specific as possible, humorous if appropriate, and very clear when explaining how they invited Christ into their lives, so that if the listener were to have no other opportunity he would know from the three-minute testimony how he can receive Christ as Savior.

> *It is vital that you be motivated by Christlike love and compassion.*

Let me strongly encourage you to memorize the four transition questions and to write and memorize your three-minute testimony. Practice them with a friend. You'll be delighted at how often these simple tools will come in handy during witnessing opportunities—and how effective they can be in helping you move from casual conversation to the gospel message.

KEEP IT SIMPLE

We don't like to admit it, but some Christians can make a gospel presentation so cumbersome that the conversation gets bogged down in minutiae. There are so many Scriptures to choose from, and so many comments we can add to those Scriptures, that it's difficult to know what to include and what to leave for later. In addition, many of us who have been believers for years may tend to think we're well beyond such simple truths as "For God so loved the world," and, as a result, we tend to overintellectualize our presentation of the gospel.

In 1951, when Vonette and I launched the ministry of Campus Crusade for Christ at UCLA, we learned very quickly that college students—whether they majored in phys ed or philosophy—weren't impressed with a complex, philosophical communication of the gospel. What impressed them was Jesus

Christ—who He is, what He did for them, and how they can know Him personally. So, during the first several years of the ministry, we gave a studied effort to making the gospel presentation as clear and simple as we could.

What I did not realize, however, was the need for consistency in one's portrayal of the gospel. During summer staff training in 1956, one of our speakers was an outstanding Christian sales consultant. He emphasized that a successful salesman must develop a clear, simple, understandable presentation that he can use over and over again. Salespeople call this the "KISS" principle, for "Keep It Simple, Stupid." Then he warned that when a salesperson grows tired of hearing himself give the same message, he develops "presentation fatigue" and tends to change his presentation around—to the detriment of his effectiveness.

His next statement startled me. "Now in sharing Christ, we need to develop a simple, understandable, logical presentation just like the successful salesman does," he told the audience. "And we need to stick with that message and not yield to presentation fatigue." I wasn't sure I agreed with him. It seemed that

> *When the meeting was over, I was still feeling irritated over the speaker's message.*

God would honor spontaneity—sharing "as the Spirit leads"—more than a prepared approach.

But if his first statement startled me, the next remark almost knocked me from my chair. "Your leader, Bill Bright, thinks he has a special message for each of the different groups he speaks to. He's ministered on skid row, in prisons, and now to college students and laypeople. Now I have never heard him speak, but

I would be willing to wager that he has only one message for everyone. Basically, he tells them all the same thing."

I squirmed in my seat and hoped that my resentment of his comments didn't show on my face. How could I, or anyone else truly committed to serving God, not be led by the Spirit to speak with originality in every situation? And how could this speaker have the audacity to embarrass me like this in front of my staff?

When the meeting was over, I was still feeling irritated over the speaker's message. But as I began to reflect on exactly what I did say in various witnessing opportunities, I asked myself: *Do I share the same basic message with everyone? Is the gospel message really that simple?*

Following the salesman's talk, I wrote out what I usually say when sharing Jesus and was amazed to discover that he had been right. Without realizing it, I had been saying basically the same thing in every witnessing situation, whether to men in prison or on skid row or to students, business leaders, or university professors. And this gospel presentation had proved effective in every setting.

What I wrote that afternoon became known as "God's Plan for Your Life," a twenty-minute presentation that I asked the staff to memorize and use in their witnessing. Within one year, our combined effectiveness in sharing Christ was dramatically multiplied. Eventually we realized the need for a shorter version, so I prepared an outline, complete with key Scripture verses and diagrams. That's how *The Four Spiritual Laws* booklet was born. It helps a reader see that just as there are physical laws that govern the physical universe, so there are spiritual laws (principles) that govern people's relationship with God. Key verses illustrate the validity of these principles, and simple diagrams help the reader apply the concepts to his own life.

We do not claim that this portrayal of the gospel is the only way to present Christ or even that it's the best way. We do hear, over and over again, that its simplicity helps cut through the minutiae to ensure that the essence of God's plan is conveyed consistently from one opportunity to another. We can testify that millions of people around the world have received Jesus Christ as Savior and Lord through this presentation. Christians worldwide, including seminary professors and pastors, have found that this little booklet has dramatically helped their witness.

POWER IN SIMPLICITY

Indeed, there is power in simplicity. My friend Frank has a twenty-year-old cousin, a computer whiz, who likes to think everything through in scientific terms. Frank's cousin mentioned to him one day that he wondered about the existence of God.

He was one of the most famous pastors in America ... but he had never personally introduced someone to Jesus.

"You know," Frank said, "I believe that just as you have physical laws that govern science, there are also spiritual laws that govern man's relationship with God. Can I show you what I'm talking about?"

Together they read through *The Four Spiritual Laws* booklet and it made sense to the young man. He eagerly prayed the suggested prayer at the end of the presentation to ask Jesus Christ into his life, then took the booklet and led his fiancée to Christ.

A few years ago I was visiting some dear friends, a doctor and his wife, and they asked if I would talk to her brother about Christ. "He's not a Christian, but he's a wonderful person," they explained. He is a respected economist and one of America's foremost businessmen. "We'll set up an appointment for you," they assured me.

A few weeks later, when I met her brother, we chatted for a few minutes about world conditions and the urgency of the moment in which we live. "You know," I offered, "I think the only one who can help us face these crises is Jesus Christ."

I watched his face for a response. "I sure agree with that," he said, nodding.

"I have something I want to show you." I pulled out a *Four Spiritual Laws* booklet, held it so he could read along, and we read through the gospel presentation. After each principle, he offered, "That makes sense. I agree with that."

We read through the suggested prayer. "Does this prayer express the desire of your heart?" I asked.

"It sure does."

"Would you like to pray it right now?"

"I sure would."

So together we prayed, asking the Lord to come into his life.

About six months later I visited him in his office in New York City. "You know, my life has made a one-hundred-eighty-degree turn since I met you," he said, smiling.

The stories go on and on. I think of a nationally known pastor who had been in the ministry for years. He attended a meeting where I spoke about walking in the Spirit, and he told me later that he now understood and was able to personalize the ministry of the Holy Spirit for the first time. About five months later he called me, late at night, rejoicing that he had just led his first person to Christ.

He was one of the most famous pastors in America, and I'm sure that thousands have received the Lord through his TV and church ministry. But he had never personally introduced someone to Jesus. His daughter had taken our training, where she learned how to use *The Four Spiritual Laws* booklet and then passed her training on to him.

In the years since we first published the booklet, tens of millions of copies have been circulated in many languages around the world. Dozens of other ministries either use the booklet or have obtained our permission to adapt it for their particular audiences. At Campus Crusade we have developed several derivative versions ourselves, each with its own distinct approach but with the same core biblical message. (Most versions are available in Christian bookstores.) In every case, the presentation of the good news remains simple and consistent.

In the next chapter I'll walk you through the booklet page by page and share tips on how you can use it effectively in a variety of situations.

———◆———

"MAY I SHOW YOU SOMETHING THAT
HAS CHANGED MY LIFE?"

———

7

Sharing Jesus

I n this chapter I'm going to bring you a condensed version of the basic evangelistic training we provide to Christian leaders and laypeople worldwide. I'll do so by walking you through the core *Four Spiritual Laws* presentation, which remains the most widely distributed gospel presentation in the world today, with the understanding that you may prefer one of the authorized derivative versions sometime in the future. If so, the training you receive in this chapter can be easily adapted to one of those alternative versions.

Over the years, those who have used this gospel presentation have realized several consistent benefits:

1. It enables you to be prepared for practically any witnessing situation.
2. It gives you confidence because you know what you are going to say and how you're going to say it.
3. It enables you to be brief.
4. It can be used to open the conversation. You can say something as simple as, "Have you heard of *The Four Spiritual Laws*?" or, "May I show you something that has changed my life?"

5. It begins on a positive note: "God loves you."
6. It presents the claims of Christ clearly.
7. It includes an invitation to receive Christ and a suggested prayer of commitment.
8. It offers suggestions for spiritual growth.
9. It emphasizes the importance of the local church.
10. It enables you to stay on the subject.
11. It gives you something tangible to leave with the person, either to reinforce the commitment he's made or to consider for a later decision.

You will also find that the more familiar you become with the core gospel message, the greater confidence you will have whenever you talk about your faith—regardless of whether you do so with an "evangelistic tool" in hand! While a booklet can serve as an excellent leave-behind piece following a conversation, your effectiveness in sharing Jesus ultimately has little to do with a booklet and everything to do with your faithfulness and how you convey the message. We have thousands of testimonies of how Christians who learned the core presentation have effectively shared it without any kind of prop whatsoever or by drawing the simple illustrations on a napkin over coffee. So while I want you to become familiar enough with the presentation to ensure simplicity and consistency, I strongly encourage you not to rely on having a booklet handy. Let the Spirit of God guide you in adapting the message to any conversational situation.

FIRST, THE BASICS

As you begin each day, ask God to make you sensitive and obedient to His leading as you interact with friends, loved ones, neighbors, coworkers, and casual encounters. Ask Him to prepare the hearts of those to whom He might lead you and to give you wisdom in sharing His love.

In addition, pray silently as you begin to share the gospel, that God would communicate through you in such a way that the hearer can make an intelligent, heartfelt decision. Be careful not to allow the presentation to become mechanical. Remember, you are not "preaching at" or "reading to" your friend; you are introducing this person to the Lord Jesus Christ! Continually pray that God will express His love through you.

Be assured that if you are walking in the Spirit, it is indeed God's will for you to share your faith with this person. Consider it a divine appointment. Remember that *success in witnessing is simply taking the initiative to share Christ in the power of the Holy Spirit and leaving the results to God.* If you obey the Spirit's prompting, no matter what the results, you cannot fail!

When you share *The Four Spiritual Laws*, simply read through the booklet. Generally, you should read aloud, holding the booklet so that the person can read along with you.

At times, the Holy Spirit will lead you to stop and explain something that may be unclear or to add a personal illustration. Normally, however, it is more effective to read through the booklet before stopping to explain or answer questions. If the person raises a question, say, "Let's remember that question and come back to it after we have finished reading the booklet."

NOW, THE GOOD NEWS

You've engaged in friendly conversation, and the topic has transitioned toward spirituality or spiritual matters. As you pull a booklet from your pocket or purse, you may wish to use one of these statements to bridge from the conversation to the gospel:

Just as there are physical laws
that govern the physical universe,
so are there spiritual laws that govern
your relationship with God.

LAW **1**

God **loves** *you and offers a*
wonderful **plan** *for your life.*

2   (References contained in this booklet should be read
in context from the Bible wherever possible.)

- "Have you heard of *The Four Spiritual Laws*? [then, open to page 2] Just as there are physical laws that govern …"
- "Could I get your opinion on something? The contents of this booklet have changed my life. It's called *The Four Spiritual Laws*, and it shows that just as there are physical laws that govern …"
- "You know, I came across a little booklet that clearly explains how we can have a personal relationship with God [or that clearly explains whatever subject you were talking about]. It demonstrates that just as there are physical laws that govern …"

If you think the person may be a Christian, but you are not sure, you could say, "Just recently I found a way to express my faith that really makes sense, and I'd like to share it with you. Have you heard of *The Four Spiritual Laws*?"

God's Love
"God so loved the world that He gave His one and only Son, that whoever believes in Him shall not perish but have eternal life" (John 3:16, NIV).

God's Plan
[Christ speaking] "I came that they might have life, and might have it abundantly" [that it might be full and meaningful] (John 10:10).

Why is it that most people are not experiencing the abundant life?

Because...

3

PAGES 2 & 3: A POSITIVE STARTING POINT—GOD LOVES YOU

Take a pen or pencil, hold the booklet so the listener can follow along with you, and begin reading. Keep a smile on your face and a smile in your voice. Make frequent eye contact and use inflection to keep life in the message. (Remember, you are sharing the best news ever!) Read at a moderate pace—neither too fast nor too slow. (Don't read the parenthetical material at the bottom of page 2.)

While many nonbelievers might expect a condemnatory assault, this presentation begins with the warmth of God's love. Pages 2 and 3 establish the important fact that God loves your friend and offers a wonderful plan for his life. A positive starting point!

LAW 2

*Man is **sinful** and **separated** from God. Therefore, he cannot know and experience God's love and plan for his life.*

Man Is Sinful

"All have sinned and fall short of the glory of God" (Romans 3:23).

Man was created to have fellowship with God; but, because of his own stubborn self-will, he chose to go his own independent way and fellowship with God was broken. This self-will, characterized by an attitude of active rebellion or passive indifference, is an evidence of what the Bible calls sin.

4

PAGES 4 & 5: WHY WE'RE SEPARATED FROM GOD

Pages 4 and 5 emphasize the reason people may not experience God's love and plan: sin. Romans 3:23 shows that sin is universal: *All* have sinned and fall short of God's ideal. Romans 6:23 declares that the consequence of sin is death, or eternal separation from God. This is the toughest part for the listener to hear, but it is essential that he understand the concept of separation from God.

Man Is Separated

"The wages of sin is death" [spiritual separation from God] (Romans 6:23).

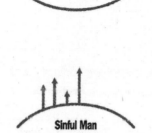

This diagram illustrates that God is holy and man is sinful. A great gulf separates the two. The arrows illustrate that man is continually trying to reach God and the abundant life through his own efforts, such as a good life, philosophy, or religion—but he inevitably fails.

The third law explains the only way to bridge this gulf...

5

You'll find the diagrams especially helpful in explaining the gospel. They give the listener a visual "hook" to grasp the truths of God's Word. Practice using them so that you can point to the diagrams while explaining the related text.

Next comes the solution to the dilemma of sin ...

LAW 3

*Jesus Christ is God's **only** provision for man's sin. Through Him you can know and experience God's love and plan for your life.*

He Died In Our Place
"God demonstrates His own love toward us, in that while we were yet sinners, Christ died for us" (Romans 5:8).

He Rose from the Dead
"Christ died for our sins…He was buried…He was raised on the third day, according to the Scriptures…He appeared to Peter, then to the twelve. After that He appeared to more than five hundred…" (1 Corinthians 15:3–6).

6

PAGES 6 & 7: THE BEST NEWS EVER!
Here it is! God's provision for people's sin—through Jesus Christ, humankind can circumvent the kingdom of darkness and enter the kingdom of light.

He Is the Only Way to God

"Jesus said to him, 'I am the way, and the truth, and the life; no one comes to the Father but through Me'" (John 14:6).

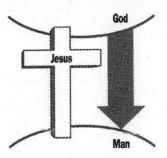

This diagram illustrates that God has bridged the gulf that separates us from Him by sending His Son, Jesus Christ, to die on the cross in our place to pay the penalty for our sins.

It is not enough just to know these three laws...   7

Pages 6 and 7 illustrate how Christ died for man's sin, rose from the dead, and is the only way to fellowship with God. God has bridged the gulf of separation through His Son, Jesus

LAW 4

*We must individually **receive** Jesus Christ as Savior and Lord; then we can know and experience God's love and plan for our lives.*

We Must Receive Christ

"As many as received Him, to them He gave the right to become children of God, even to those who believe in His name" (John 1:12).

We Receive Christ Through Faith

"By grace you have been saved through faith; and that not of yourselves, it is the gift of God; not as a result of works that no one should boast" (Ephesians 2:8,9).

When We Receive Christ, We Experience a New Birth

(Read John 3:1–8.)

8

PAGES 8 & 9: PERSONALIZING THE GOOD NEWS

These pages emphasize the fact that it is not enough to merely give intellectual assent to the first three principles. One must personally receive Jesus Christ as Savior and Lord in order to know and live out God's love and plan. Here the listener is shown how to receive Christ and what it involves.

Pay special attention to the two circles at the bottom of page 9. These are especially effective in helping your friend acknowledge where he or she stands with God. Recently I asked Lance, a skycap at an airport, to look over *The Four Spiritual Laws* booklet while I gathered my luggage. When all

We Receive Christ Through Personal Invitation

[Christ speaking] "Behold, I stand at the door and knock; if any one hears My voice and opens the door, I will come in to him" (Revelation 3:20).

Receiving Christ involves turning to God from self (repentance) and trusting Christ to come into our lives to forgive our sins and to make us what He wants us to be. Just to agree **intellectually** that Jesus Christ is the Son of God and that He died on the cross for our sins is not enough. Nor is it enough to have an **emotional** experience. We receive Jesus Christ by **faith**, as an act of the **will**.

These two circles represent two kinds of lives:

Self-Directed Life
S – Self is on the throne
† – Christ is outside the life
● – Interests are directed by self, often resulting in discord and frustration

Christ-Directed Life
† – Christ is in the life and on the throne
S – Self is yielding to Christ
● – Interests are directed by Christ, resulting in harmony with God's plan

Which circle best represents your life?
Which circle would you like to have represent your life?

my suitcases were accounted for, I asked him, "Which circle represents your life?"

"The one on the left," Lance replied.

"Which circle would you like to represent your life?"

"The one on the right," he said, resolutely.

Within just a few moments, Lance had discerned his standing with God and realized that he wanted Christ as his Lord and Savior. Together, we stood aside from the airport bustle, and Lance prayed the suggested prayer. We shook hands, and he wrote down his mailing address for me, rejoicing at his newfound relationship with the Lord.

Learn the circle diagram well. It helps your friend visualize the real difference between the self-directed person and the Christ-directed person, and it encourages him to identify exactly where he stands. You'll find that it comes in handy in a variety of situations. Some people have even used the diagram successfully to *begin* a conversation about spiritual things.

Next is the all-important opportunity for your friend to make the biggest decision of his life ...

The following explains how you can receive Christ:

**You Can Receive Christ Right Now
by Faith Through Prayer**
(Prayer is talking with God)
God knows your heart and is not so concerned with your words as He is with the attitude of your heart. The following is a suggested prayer:

> Lord Jesus, I need You. Thank You for dying on the cross for my sins. I open the door of my life and receive You as my Savior and Lord. Thank You for forgiving my sins and giving me eternal life. Take control of the throne of my life. Make me the kind of person You want me to be.

Does this prayer express the desire of your heart?

If it does, I invite you to pray this prayer right now, and Christ will come into your life, as He promised.

10

PAGE 10: A SUGGESTED PRAYER

One receives Christ not by prayer, but by faith. Prayer, however, is a tangible, conscious way of expressing faith and of opening the door of one's life to Jesus. The suggested prayer on this page contains several important acknowledgments and commitments on the part of the listener, so go through it thoughtfully.

Then come the two most important questions you will ask during the entire conversation:

1. "John, does this prayer express the desire of your heart?"
2. "Would you like to pray it right now?"

You will be tempted to be shy at this crucial juncture, but this is where the listener needs your confident, calm leadership. When he says yes, have him repeat the prayer after you, a phrase at a time. (We'll discuss in the next chapter what to do if the listener is hesitant or says no.) When you have finished praying together, take a moment to congratulate him. This is cause for celebration! Then say, "Now I'm going to ask you a few questions just so you understand what has just happened …" and proceed to page 11.

How to Know That Christ Is in Your Life

Did you receive Christ into your life? According to His promise in Revelation 3:20, where is Christ right now in relation to you? Christ said He would come into your life. Would He mislead you? On what authority do you know God has answered your prayer? (The trustworthiness of God Himself and His Word.)

The Bible Promises Eternal Life to All Who Receive Christ

"God has given us eternal life, and this life is in His Son. He who has the Son has the life; he who does not have the Son of God does not have the life. These things I have written to you who believe in the name of the Son of God, in order that you may **know** that you have eternal life" (1 John 5:11–13).

Thank God often that Christ is in your life and that He will never leave you (Hebrews 13:5). You can know on the basis of His promise that Christ lives in you and that you have eternal life from the very moment you invite Him in. He will not deceive you.

11

PAGE 11: ASSURANCE OF SALVATION

Ask your new brother or sister in Christ the questions at the top of page 11 to help underscore God's promise of salvation. Your friend can be assured that, because God and His Word are reliable, Christ is now in his or her life.

And, because God and His Word are reliable, your friend now has *eternal* life. Read through 1 John 5:11–13 to affirm this fact. You might ask at this point, "John, according to God's Word, when you die, what is going to happen to you?" (John will have eternal life in heaven according to 1 John 5:11–13; John 3:16; Romans 6:23.)

An important reminder...

Do Not Depend on Feelings
The promise of God's Word, the Bible—not our feelings—is our authority. The Christian lives by faith (trust) in the trustworthiness of God Himself and His Word. This train diagram illustrates the relationship among **fact** (God and His Word), **faith** (our trust in God and His Word), and **feeling** (the result of our faith and obedience). (Read John 14:21.)

The train will run with or without the caboose. However, it would be useless to attempt to pull the train by the caboose. In the same way, as Christians we do not depend on feelings or emotions, but we place our faith (trust) in the trustworthiness of God and the promises of His Word.

12

PAGE 12: "YOU MAY NOT FEEL DIFFERENT"

Page 12 addresses the question of feelings. Some people have dramatic conversions while for others it's a calm, quiet decision. Continue reading through the text, emphasizing how the train diagram illustrates the proper perspective on feelings.

Some days our feelings might be high while on other days they may be low. But the FACT (timeless truth) of God's trustworthiness, as conveyed in His Word, remains constant. In other words, our trust should not be in how we feel at any given time, but in the FACT provided by the Holy Bible. FEELINGS are a result of our FAITH but should not be a determining *cause* of our faith.

Now That You Have Received Christ

The moment you received Christ by faith, as an act of the will, many things happened, including the following:

- Christ came into your life (Revelation 3:20; Colossians 1:27).

- Your sins were forgiven (Colossians 1:14).

- You became a child of God (John 1:12).

- You received eternal life (John 5:24).

- You began the great adventure for which God created you (John 10:10; 2 Corinthians 5:17; 1 Thessalonians 5:18).

Can you think of anything more wonderful that could happen to you than receiving Christ? Would you like to thank God in prayer right now for what He has done for you? By thanking God, you demonstrate your faith.

To enjoy your new life to the fullest...

13

PAGE 13: SNEAK PREVIEW OF THE NEW LIFE

Page 13 is a quick overview of what transpired in your friend's heart when he received Christ. You'll want to encourage your friend to take the booklet home, dust off a Bible, and look up each of the references in context to affirm that God has indeed worked a miracle of love in his life. If time allows, have prayer together as suggested at the bottom of page 13, thanking God for what He has done.

Suggestions for Christian Growth

Spiritual growth results from trusting Jesus Christ. "The righteous man shall live by faith" (Galatians 3:11). A life of faith will enable you to trust God increasingly with every detail of your life, and to practice the following:

G   *Go* to God in prayer daily (John 15:7).

R   *Read* God's Word daily (Acts 17:11); begin with the Gospel of John.

O   *Obey* God moment by moment (John 14:21).

W   *Witness* for Christ by your life and words (Matthew 4:19; John 15:8).

T   *Trust* God for every detail of your life (1 Peter 5:7).

H   *Holy Spirit*—allow Him to control and empower your daily life and witness (Galatians 5:16,17; Acts 1:8).

14

PAGES 14 & 15: SUGGESTIONS FOR GROWTH

Here is a minicourse on what new Christians can do to begin growing in their newfound relationship with Jesus Christ. Encourage your friend to study these on his own.

Fellowship in a Good Church

God's Word instructs us not to forsake "the assembling of ourselves together" (Hebrews 10:25). Several logs burn brightly together, but put one aside on the cold hearth and the fire goes out. So it is with your relationship with other Christians.

If you do not belong to a church, do not wait to be invited. Take the initiative; call the pastor of a nearby church where Christ is honored and His Word is preached. Start this week, and make plans to attend regularly.

Special Materials Are Available for Christian Growth

If you have come to know Christ personally through this presentation of the gospel, helpful materials for Christian growth are available to you. For more information, write Campus Crusade for Christ, 100 Lake Hart Drive 2100, Orlando, FL 32832-0100.

15

We especially emphasize the importance of finding a good local church. Every Christian needs fellowship with other believers who love the Lord and His inspired Word and who encourage and strengthen each other's walk with God.

Provided at the bottom of page 15 is an address anyone can write to for materials to help them move forward in their new faith. I also heartily recomend that new Christians read "The Joy of Knowing God" series, starting with *The Joy of Trusting God: Character You Can Count On* (available in bookstores and through our publisher, www.cookministries.com).

AFTER THE PRESENTATION

I cannot stress enough the importance of follow-up for a new Christian, and in chapter 9 we will look at the essentials you need to know. Immediately after a friend receives Christ, however, there is some vital ground you'll want to cover as well.

1. Give him the copy of *The Four Spiritual Laws* booklet and encourage him to read through it again that night.

2. Exchange phone numbers and/or e-mail addresses.

3. Try to set an appointment to meet over coffee within the next twenty-four to forty-eight hours. (If this doesn't work out, use your first phone or e-mail contact to reinvite him to coffee.)

4. Encourage him to read the first three chapters of the gospel of John that night before going to bed.

Note: If the new believer is of the opposite sex, I strongly recommend that you have a trusted friend of the same gender do the follow-up. I have often told women, for example, "I know a sharp Christian woman whose background is very similar to yours. Would you mind if I had her contact you?" This precaution will help prevent misunderstandings or confusing emotions.

PULLING IT ALL TOGETHER

In our training conferences we pair the conferees to practice delivery of *The Four Spiritual Laws* one-on-one. Let me encourage you to find a friend with whom you can shake out the initial jitters you might feel as you begin to present the booklet aloud. Have the person be a "friendly listener" at this point, posing no objections or questions. The aim is to get you comfortable with the basic presentation. In the next chapter, we'll look at how to handle some potential questions and smoke screens that might come your way.

WHEN IN DOUBT ABOUT WHAT TO SAY,
LET GOD'S WORD DO THE TALKING.

8

Handling Objections, Hostility, Questions, and Resistance

I don't believe in God, I don't believe in the Bible, and I don't believe in Christ and Christianity."

Ken's eyes flared at me from under the blond hair on his forehead as he cornered me following a campus lecture on the deity of Jesus Christ. He was a philosophy student, and I learned later from some other students that Ken seemed to delight in tearing Christianity apart. He seemed ready to tear *me* apart that night.

I put my hand on his shoulder and asked, "Why don't we sit down and talk?"

As we pulled two chairs together for conversation, I quickly asked God for wisdom. He seemed to be reminding me: *Don't argue. Ask questions to find out why he feels the way he does.*

"Tell me what you don't believe about the Bible," I began.

"I just don't believe it. It's filled with all kinds of contradictions and myths." Ken slouched back in his chair, his arms folded tightly across his chest.

"Have you ever read it?"

"Oh yes. Cover to cover."

I handed Ken my Bible. "Can you show me what troubles you?"

"Well, there are thousands of contradictions ..." His voice faded as he thumbed at the pages.

"Ken, if you'll show me one of the problems or contradictions that trouble you, maybe we can talk about it."

By now Ken was flustered. He leaned forward, elbows on knees, and leafed through the Bible halfheartedly, realizing he couldn't produce evidence to back up his contentions.

> *"Ken, I think I understand how you're feeling," I said.*

"You say you've read the Bible, Ken?"

"Yes."

"How long ago did you read it?"

"Some time ago."

"How long? How old were you when you read it?"

"Oh ... I guess I was twelve."

"Are you letting opinions you formed when you were twelve years old influence your lifelong decisions? Ken, I think I understand how you're feeling. In my days of agnosticism, I would often parrot what I had heard other agnostics say without checking the facts for myself. But do I discern, Ken, that the real reason you've come to me tonight is that you really want to know God personally?"

He leaned back in his chair. His cheeks bellowed as he exhaled loudly. "Yes," he sighed. "I do."

"Would you like to examine what Jesus Christ himself said about how to know God?"

He nodded. Together, we went through *The Four Spiritual Laws* booklet, and Ken invited Christ into his life. We talked for quite a while about his new commitment, prayed together, then rose to leave.

"Mr. Bright—" Ken stopped me, his hand on my arm.

"Yes?"

His blue eyes had been transformed from hostility to peace. "Thank you. Thank you for not letting my big mouth prevent you from showing me the truth."

Despite Ken's loud protests and seeming hostility, God had special plans for him that night. Frankly, I don't enjoy confrontations, but I have learned from many experiences that, like Ken, people who respond with the greatest hostility toward Christ are sometimes the most ready to receive Him. Deep down, they are crying out for help. Their visible belligerence is only a smoke screen to hide their hurt and hunger.

"OVER MY DEAD BODY!"

I recall an invitation from a group of Christian students at UCLA to speak in their fraternity. Their president, who was known as one of the campus's heaviest drinkers and loudest critics of Christianity, protested: "Over my dead body!"

"Okay," joked several of his brothers, all hefty athletes. "Over your dead body."

They let him live, and he attended the fraternity meeting. After my talk I invited anyone who wanted to become a Christian to see me afterward. Almost all of the men gathered around me—and he was one of the first to ask for an appointment.

When we were alone, he confided, "Because I'm always the life of the party, drinking and putting on an act, most of my friends think I'm happy. But I'm probably the most miserable guy on this campus. I need God."

To the utter amazement of his fraternity brothers, this young man received Christ two days later, turned his life around, and became one of the campus's most active students for the Lord.

"ANOTHER RELIGIOUS FANATIC"

A series of meetings at the University of Houston brought me face-to-face with another philosophy major, Benjamin—an older student renowned for his intellect and for his anti-God activism on campus. Our campus director invited Benjamin to visit with me at a coffee shop after a long day of meetings. Benjamin, I learned later, had welcomed the opportunity to "debate another religious fanatic."

The three of us visited for more than an hour, but it was a classic case of noncommunication. Benjamin would give lengthy quotes from atheistic philosophers. When he stopped for breath, I would tell him how much God loves him. He would then declare that God couldn't exist, to which I replied how I had felt the same way as an agnostic before Jesus changed my life.

I had been up and running since before dawn. Exhausted, I suggested we call it a night.

"Would you mind dropping me off at my dorm?" Benjamin asked us.

I got in the backseat, thinking I'd get a start on some much-needed sleep. But before we pulled out of the parking lot, Benjamin turned around in the front passenger's seat and said, "Mr. Bright, everything you said tonight hit me in the heart. I'd like to receive Christ right now."

Needless to say, I was no longer sleepy.

Benjamin had given no indication that he was close to

accepting the claims of Christ. There had been no positive response during our awkward conversation. I hadn't been what you'd call profound in my verbal witness. But the Holy Spirit had prepared this young intellectual's heart and had used me, in spite of my weariness, to penetrate the facade.

LOOK FOR THE UNDERLYING MEANING

As you share Christ with others faithfully, you will occasionally encounter hostility, questions, and resistance. Be sensitive to the leading of the Holy Spirit. There is a time to bring an end to a conversation, give the listener something to read, and encourage him to invite Christ into his life when ready.

But you will also find that, in many cases, your friend's initial resistance really signifies that he wants to know more—that his questions indicate a sincere interest in overcoming some doubts. Quite often, initial hostility is actually a mask that hides a deep-down desire to settle things with God.

The purpose of this chapter is to help you guide a friend through such smoke screens, so he can focus on the person of Jesus Christ and make an intelligent decision. Before we address specific objections you might encounter, let's establish some important guidelines.

NEVER ARGUE

Remember, your mission is to proclaim the good news—not to win an argument. Let the unconditional love of God pervade your words, your tone of voice, and your facial expressions. Answer questions and ask questions, but do not argue.

DON'T TRY TO REASON WITHIN
YOUR FRIEND'S EXPERTISE

I studied philosophy, but I would have dug quite a hole for myself if I had tried to reason philosophically with Ken or Benjamin. I studied science, but I wouldn't fare well if I tried to reason from science with a scientist. So I try to stay focused on the person of Jesus Christ—His love, His death and resurrection, His gift of eternal life.

REMEMBER WHAT GOD
HAS COMMISSIONED YOU TO DO

Your task is only to proclaim; it is God's task to convert. Share the claims of Christ thoroughly and answer questions calmly, to the best of your ability. Give the listener ample opportunity to respond. In many cases he will respond favorably. But if he does not, you have planted a seed—and you can trust God with the results.

❖

Your task is only to proclaim; it is God's task to convert.

Remember: *Successful witnessing is simply taking the initiative to share Christ in the power of the Holy Spirit and leaving the results to God.*

APPEAL TO INTELLECTUAL INTEGRITY

No one wants to be "intellectually dishonest," but this is precisely the error many people make when resisting God's Word: It is the one thing they refuse to investigate objectively. By appealing to their intellectual integrity, you can help them see that they should indeed give the gospel a fair hearing.

When Questions Might Come

Questions, resistance, and objections may occur in one of three places during your conversation:

- during preliminary conversation;
- during the presentation, particularly regarding the circle diagram on page 9; or
- following the reading of the suggested prayer on page 10.

If an objection comes up during preliminary conversation, you can deal with it briefly and then actually use it as a bridge to the gospel presentation. For example, your friend states, "I don't feel that God loves me after the things I've done." You could reply, "You know, it's amazing—I've discovered that God loves us in spite of what we've done. In fact, I've come across a little booklet that explains it beautifully—would you like to see what the Bible says about God's love?"

If an objection is raised while you're going through the booklet, remember to graciously defer the question since it's quite possible that the objection will be answered within the presentation. However, in the rare event that your friend is obviously annoyed and doesn't want you to continue, then stop and apologize: "I'm sorry if I have offended you. Here, why don't you keep the booklet and read through it yourself when you're ready?"

> ❖
>
> *"I don't feel that God loves me after the things I've done."*

If questions or objections surface after you've invited your friend to pray the suggested prayer, *now* is the time to patiently address each question. You have laid the foundation by showing the four biblical principles. If his questions weren't answered by the context of the presentation, try to answer them now. Never push or rush a decision for Christ. When you sense that the listener's questions have been answered, you can gently ask, "Is there anything now that would prevent you from receiving Christ? How about doing it right now?"

THE 30-DAY EXPERIMENT

The person who says "I don't believe," is usually more of a candidate for the kingdom than one who says "I don't care." I have found that, in many cases, those who declare that they don't believe in God, the Bible, or the deity of Christ have been hurt and have emotional scars. Perhaps they were offended by an overly strict parent, an immoral Christian leader, or another adult who talked the Christian life but didn't live it. If this is not the case, it's possible that they are on some sort of prideful, intellectual kick.

Whether they profess atheism, agnosticism, militant humanism, or honest doubt, an appeal to their intellectual integrity through the "30-Day Experiment" can bring dramatic results.

They subconsciously hope I'll see through their facade and help them.

How does the experiment work?

A Christian student was dating a man who was rigorously antagonistic toward God. She asked me if I would talk with him, and when I arrived, he was absolutely furious.

"I don't care about your God," he fumed, "and I really don't care to talk to you." He added a few other choice comments that I cannot repeat.

I felt awkward, caught in the middle. Apparently she had not told him or even asked him about my visit.

"Look, I'm sorry," I apologized. "I don't normally become

involved in the middle of something like this. But before I go, I want to say this: You are dating a wonderful young Christian woman. You can ruin her life, and you have no right to have anything more to do with her unless you let God take hold of your life."

He wouldn't even talk to me. His face was so red with anger that I can still feel the heat he generated. I moved to the edge of my chair to get up. "I want to leave you with this thought: You say you don't believe in God or the Bible. I'm going to ask you to perform an experiment, as a matter of intellectual integrity.

"Read the Bible every day, starting with the gospel of John. One hour a day for thirty days. And every day begin your reading with a prayer: *God, if You exist, and if Jesus Christ is Your revelation to man and He truly died for my sins, I want to know You personally.*

"If you pray that prayer every day and read the Bible for an hour objectively— as an honest seeker of truth—I think you'll know what I'm talking about."

He did not respond to my suggestion. About four months later his girlfriend received a letter from him. He had been traveling in Europe and had begun to read the Bible. He wrote his girlfriend: *I'm ecstatic! I performed the 30-Day Experiment your friend told me about, and I now know why you're so excited about Christ. I, too, have received Him as my Savior and Lord!*

"WOULD YOU PERFORM AN EXPERIMENT?"

At the University of Colorado a young man present at an evangelistic breakfast announced, "This God business is a lot of nonsense." Of course, I had learned that often when people like him come to me, they're actually hungry for God. In many cases, I've discovered, they subconsciously hope I'll see through their facade and help them.

"Are you an honest person?" I asked.

"Of course I am."

"Would you perform an experiment?"

"Like what?"

"A scientist goes into the laboratory to do research without preconceived ideas. He goes with an open mind and considers all truth objectively. Would you be willing to perform an experiment for thirty days, as a matter of intellectual integrity?"

I described the 30-Day Experiment. "Well, I could do that," he said, shrugging.

"What are you doing today?" I probed.

"It happens to be my free day—that's why I'm here."

"I know you'll want to be intellectually honest about this, just like an objective scientist. Why don't you take the whole day and go read the gospel of John. Read it and pray that if Jesus Christ is God, and if He died for your sins, He will come into your life and be your Savior and Lord."

That evening I was speaking to a group of several hundred students. As I began, I looked out over the crowd. There, right in the middle of the auditorium, was this young man— beaming at me with a countenance that could have lighted the whole auditorium.

I could hardly wait until the meeting was over, and when I finished, he darted through the crowd to meet me. "I did it," he said, grinning. "I did what you told me. I read the first, second, third, and fourth chapters of John." I'll never forget his next statement: "I was in the eighth chapter when Jesus stepped out of the pages of the Bible into my heart."

In almost any situation where hostility, unbelief, or doubt is expressed, you can appeal to one's intellectual integrity by proposing the 30-Day Experiment. The principle: *When in doubt about what to say, let God's Word do the talking.*

OTHER QUESTIONS AND SMOKE SCREENS

Below is a quick tour of some objections that may arise as you share Jesus. I have provided responses that have proven effective.

"*I'M AN ATHEIST; THERE IS NO GOD*"

"John, do you know everything there is to know?"

"Of course not. Even Einstein only scratched the surface of knowledge."

> *"Jesus stepped out of the pages of the Bible into my heart."*

"Of all the knowledge in the world, what percent do you think you know? Eighty percent?"

"Oh no! I'd do well to understand 1 or 2 percent."

"All right. But let's assume that you knew 80 percent. Isn't it at all possible that God could exist in that 20 percent of all knowledge you don't know?"

"*I BELIEVE GOD IS IN ALL MEN*"

"Nancy, do you think Jesus Christ was a liar?"

"Oh no. He was probably the most moral person who ever lived."

"If He wasn't a liar, was He a deluded lunatic?"

"No—why do you ask that?"

"Well, there are only three choices. If He wasn't a liar, and if He wasn't a lunatic, then what He said had to be truth. As a matter of intellectual integrity, wouldn't you want to consider what He taught about man's relationship to God?"

"Jesus Was a Great Teacher but Not God"

Use the Liar/Lunatic approach illustrated above. Then, when explaining the three choices, say, "If He wasn't a liar, and if He wasn't a lunatic, then what He said about Himself had to be truth. He had to be who He said He was. As a matter of intellectual integrity, wouldn't you want to consider what He taught about His relationship to God?"

"If We're Good People, We'll Go to Heaven"

Again, utilize the Liar/Lunatic approach. When explaining the third choice, say, "… then what He said had to be truth. As a matter of intellectual integrity, wouldn't you want to consider what He taught about eternal life?" Then, when going through the gospel presentation, place special emphasis on Ephesians 2:8–9: "For by grace you have been saved through faith, and that not of yourselves; it is the gift of God, not of works, lest anyone should boast" (NKJV).

"I Don't Believe the Bible"

"Let me ask you a question. The main message of the Bible, which is unquestionably the most important literary work in history, is how a person may have eternal life. Do you understand what the Bible teaches about this?"

"I Don't Believe in Eternal Life"

"I'm not asking you what you believe, but what you understand. Don't you agree that it would be intellectually dishonest to reject the world's most important book without understanding even its main message?"

Most people at this point will guess that the way to have eternal life is through being and doing good things.

"John, that's an interesting answer, but it's the opposite of what the Bible teaches. Now I know you want to be objective and exercise intellectual integrity. Don't you think the more intellectual approach would be to investigate what the Scriptures actually teach on this matter? Then you can make an intelligent decision whether to accept or reject it."

"I'VE SEEN TOO MANY HYPOCRITES"

"Nancy, any time we look at men instead of God we'll see sin and weakness. Christians are still human, and they'll still fail because God gives them freedom to choose whether He's in control or they are in control of their lives.

"Someone said, 'The church is not a retail store, it's a repair shop.' That's so true—becoming a Christian doesn't mean we're perfect, just forgiven. We'll still sin, but as we allow God to control us, sin will become less and less appealing.

"But the important question is not 'What about the hypocrites?' Rather, it is 'What about *my* sin and God's provision for it?' Would you like to investigate what Jesus Christ said about God's relationship to you?"

"I GO TO CHURCH AND SERVE ON A COMMITTEE"

"I realize that you have done all these things. But have you ever personally received Jesus Christ as your Savior and Lord?"

"I'm not sure."

"Would you like to be sure?"

"I'm Not Interested"

"I understand. There may come a time in the future when spiritual matters *do* become important to you. May I give you something that has meant a lot to me in this regard? Why don't you take it home and read it and see what you think?" (Write your name, address, and phone number on the back of the booklet and give it to him. Challenge him to undertake the 30-Day Experiment.)

Responses to "Which Circle Represents Your Life?"

If your friend responds, "The circle on the left," simply continue by asking the next question: "Which circle would you *like to* have represent your life?"

If he says, "I'm not sure," or "I'm in-between," or if he remains silent, simply continue by asking the next question: "Which circle would you *like to* have represent your life?"

If he responds, "The circle on the right," you might say, "Great! I'm delighted to hear that Christ is in your life. Maybe you could use this to share your faith in Christ with someone else. Let me show you how it drives home the crucial point."

- If he is a Christian, the rest of the presentation will help him learn how to present the claims of Christ to others.
- If he is not a Christian, he may realize it after going through the suggested prayer.
- After reading the suggested prayer, ask, "Have you ever received Christ in the way this prayer expresses?" If he has, encourage him to use this presentation to witness to others. If he has not, give him the opportunity to invite Christ into his life right then, "to be sure without a doubt that you have received Christ into your life."

"WHICH CIRCLE WOULD YOU LIKE TO HAVE REPRESENT YOUR LIFE?"

If your friend says, "The circle on the right," simply continue with the transition at the top of page 10: "The following explains how you can receive Christ."

If he answers that he's not sure, or if he remains silent, continue with the transition at the top of page 10.

If he responds, "The circle on the left," don't let it rattle you. Stay positive and loving. You could say, "John, at some time in your life you may want to receive Christ. Let me show you how you can invite Christ into your life, so you'll know, when that time comes. Sound fair?" Continue reading through the prayer.

"DOES THIS PRAYER EXPRESS YOUR HEART?"

If your friend says yes, say, "Would you like to repeat the prayer after me as I read it a sentence at a time?" If he feels uncomfortable about praying aloud, you could ask him to read through the prayer silently, praying in his heart.

Be sensitive to his comfort level at this point. In many cases, if a person shows hesitancy to pray along with me, I'll give him the booklet and encourage him to pray the prayer silently. Or, if he does not wish to do so, I encourage him to pray this prayer when he gets home. Many people have contacted me by phone or letter to let me know that they have done so.

If he says he would like to pray the prayer at home, say, "That would be fine. Many people like to do so in privacy. Let's just take a moment to preview what will happen in your life when you receive Christ tonight." Go through the bottom section of page 11 and the five points on page 13.

If your friend says no, maintain a positive and loving spirit. Again, you could say, "It's an important decision, and I'm glad you're not taking it lightly. Let me show you what would happen if you asked Christ to come into your life." Go through the bottom section of page 11 and the five points on page 13.

"I'M NOT READY"

"It *is* an important decision—the most important one you'll make in your entire life because it affects how you'll spend eternity. So I appreciate the fact that you're not taking it lightly. But there may come a time when you are ready—would you take this booklet and read it so that, when the time comes, you'll know how to receive Christ?"

PLANTING THE SEED

Never let objections intimidate you. Handle them in the best way you can, and see if you can gently guide the conversation back to the suggested prayer. If the response is still negative, put your name, address, and phone number on the back of the booklet, and leave it with your friend. Quite often, a hesitant hearer will reread the booklet and receive Christ in the privacy of his home.

Challenge him to do the 30-Day Experiment. Then pray for him and leave the results to God. You have planted a seed for God to nurture in His perfect timing.

When Chuck was a senior journalism major at the University of Missouri, he shared Christ with Dave, a promising freshman journalism student. Dave considered the gospel message carefully but responded, "I'm not ready for this kind of thing."

Well, I've planted a seed, Chuck thought as he prayed for Dave. Over the next year he dropped by Dave's room often to discuss journalism and sports. But when Chuck graduated, Dave was still not a Christian.

In Dave's sophomore year he attended a campus lecture by Josh McDowell, who again emphasized the need for a personal relationship with Jesus Christ. By this time, Dave was ready—he invited Christ into his life and later began studying the Bible with a group of Christian students.

God moves in mysterious ways. Dave graduated with his journalism degree and joined the staff of Campus Crusade for Christ, where he served as editor of one of our magazines. One of Dave's right-hand colleagues was Chuck, the young man who "planted the seed" years ago. Together, they impacted thousands of lives for Christ as the magazine went to more than one hundred thousand homes every other month.

So never let hostility, questions, and objections discourage you. God is sovereign—He has given you the duty and the privilege of sharing Jesus faithfully, intelligently, and lovingly—and you can leave the results to Him. Your task is simply to obey; His is to change the hearts of those with whom you share.

I PRAY FOR YOU CONSTANTLY, ASKING GOD,
THE GLORIOUS FATHER OF OUR LORD JESUS CHRIST, TO
GIVE YOU SPIRITUAL WISDOM AND UNDERSTANDING SO
THAT YOU MIGHT GROW IN YOUR KNOWLEDGE OF GOD. I
PRAY THAT YOUR HEARTS WILL BE FLOODED
WITH LIGHT SO THAT YOU CAN UNDERSTAND THE
WONDERFUL FUTURE HE HAS PROMISED
TO THOSE HE CALLED.

EPHESIANS 1:16–18

9

Live It!

The apostle Paul took seriously our Lord's Great Commission. To the Colossians he wrote, "So everywhere we go, we tell everyone about Christ. We warn them and teach them with all the wisdom God has given us, for we want to present them to God, perfect in their relationship to Christ" (1:28).

The early church grew so dramatically because evangelism, discipleship, and spiritual multiplication were intertwined in everything the Lord Jesus and the apostle Paul did. And key to presenting "each one to God, perfect because of what Christ has done for each of them" (Colossians 1:28 TLB), is following up the new believer's decision for Christ with helpful instruction and support to help him grow.

"Follow-up" is a relatively contemporary term that describes the vital, initial stages of discipleship. Ideally, follow-up begins within twenty-four hours and is done by either the person who led the new Christian to the Lord or by a trusted Christian delegated to the task. The discipler's job during follow-up is to:

- provide encouragement, answer questions, and lend prayer support;
- help the new believer understand and further commit to the lordship of Jesus Christ;
- network the new convert with other Christians and a Bible-teaching church fellowship; and
- help wean this "babe in Christ" from milk to solid food through a systematic beginning Bible study and training in how to share his new faith.

GET TOGETHER SOON

You will recall that whenever someone receives Christ with you, it is important to get his address and phone number. If you live in close proximity, try to set an appointment to get together the next day (two days at most). Explain that you want to give him more information that will help him begin his new life. Encourage him to take *The Four Spiritual Laws* booklet home and reread it that night to affirm God's love for him and the decision he has made. In addition, he should try to read the first three chapters of the gospel of John prior to getting with you again. Ask him to bring any questions he might have. (If the new Christian does not reside in your locale, you can still conduct meaningful follow-up via phone, e-mail, and snail mail.)

There is a wide variety of helpful follow-up materials you can use with a new convert. The book you hold is part of our new series "The Joy of Knowing God"—my ten most vital Christian-growth messages for new as well as experienced believers. Each book comes with a companion audio CD, read by a well-known Christian, and a readers' guide for group interaction or personal reflection. Getting a new believer started in this series is an excellent way to encourage knowledge of God and personal spiritual growth. The titles are:

1. *The Joy of Trusting God: Character You Can Count On*
2. *The Joy of Finding Jesus: He Will Meet Your Every Need*
3. *The Joy of Spirit-Filled Living: The Power to Succeed*
4. *The Joy of Intimacy with God: Rekindling Your First Love*
5. *The Joy of Total Forgiveness: The Key to Guilt-Free Living*
6. *The Joy of Active Prayer: Your Access to the Almighty*
7. *The Joy of Faithful Obedience: Your Way to God's Best*
8. *The Joy of Supernatural Thinking: Believing God for the Impossible*
9. *The Joy of Dynamic Giving: Investing for Eternal Blessings*
10. *The Joy of Sharing Jesus: You Have a Story to Tell*

The entire series is available in Christian bookstores everywhere or directly from the publisher, Cook Communications Ministries, at www.cookministries.com.

THE FIRST FOLLOW-UP

The first meeting (or phone call) is a time to reinforce the significance of what God has done (and is doing) in the life of the new Christian. Here is what should be covered:

1. Questions the new believer may have.
2. The relation of FEELINGS to FACT and FAITH. Review the train diagram on page 12 of *The Four Spiritual Laws* booklet.
3. Assurance of salvation. Ask, "Where is Jesus Christ right now in relation to you?" Review Revelation 3:20. Ask, "If you were to die tonight, do you know without a doubt that you would go to heaven?" Review 1 John 5:11–13. Ask, "Will Jesus Christ ever leave you?" Review Hebrews 13:5.

4. Walk through the five FACTS on page 13, looking up and reading together the Scriptures that support each point:
   - Christ has come into your life (see Revelation 3:20; Colossians 1:27).
   - Your sins have been forgiven (see Colossians 1:14).
   - You have become a child of God (see John 1:12).
   - You have received eternal life (see John 5:24).
   - You have begun the great adventure for which God created you (see John 10:10; 2 Corinthians 5:17; 1 Thessalonians 5:18).

5. If you have not done so already, encourage your friend to begin reading the gospel of John upon rising in the morning or before going to sleep at night. Introduce it as a historical account of the life of Jesus Christ and what His life means to us.

6. Give your friend either *The Joy of Trusting God* or *The Joy of Finding Jesus* from "The Joy of Knowing God" series. Encourage him to read and underline passages in the book, noting any questions he may have. Listening to the CD version will reinforce what he reads. Invite him to get together within a week or so to go through the readers' guide questions with you.

> *"Follow-up" is a relatively contemporary term that describes the vital, initial stages of discipleship.*

7. Pray together, thanking God for the salvation and new life He has brought to your friend.

THE SECOND FOLLOW-UP

When possible, your second follow-up session should be within three days of the first. Frequent contact at the beginning of the disciple-building process will help your friend gain positive momentum and also help prevent doubts, questions, and daily problems from overwhelming him.

1. Pray together, asking God to bless your time of fellowship.
2. Find out how your friend is doing in reading the gospel of John. You might ask, "What are the most meaningful truths you have discovered in your reading?" Do your best to answer his questions. If you don't know an answer, be honest and say so; promise to call or e-mail an answer to him as soon as possible. Encourage him to continue reading God's Word.
3. Ask how he's doing with the first "Joy of Knowing God" book and CD you gave him. Address any questions he may have; then choose and discuss some of the readers' guide questions.
4. If he lives in your locale, invite him to church with you next Sunday. Offer a ride, and either take him to lunch or invite him home for lunch afterward.
5. If you're doing follow-up over a long distance, mail your new believer the recommended book and discuss it by phone or e-mail. Encourage him to write you with further questions and regular reports on how he's doing spiritually. Through your pastor or other reliable contacts, locate a good church in your friend's locale, and encourage him to attend. You can drop the pastor of that church a note encouraging him to invite your friend to the next Sunday's activities.
6. Pray together, and if he'd like to, continue meeting. If so, set another appointment for approximately one week later.

SUBSEQUENT FOLLOW-UP

After the first one or two meetings I encourage you to continue regular contact with your friend, whether you meet together or phone or e-mail messages of encouragement. See if you can get him involved in a small-group Bible study in which participants also pray for and encourage each other. Continue to give or send materials that will help him understand and grow in his newfound faith. However you maintain contact, keep in mind three overarching practices of effective discipleship.

1. LEAD BY EXAMPLE

Let your personal enthusiasm for God and His Word be evident in your daily walk. We cannot expect others to become avid students of the Word unless *we* are avid students of the Word. We cannot expect them to lead others to Christ unless they see us leading others to Christ. By example, you can role-model practical Christian living: victory over circumstances; faith in troubled times; a godly, moral, Christ-centered lifestyle; and love, joy, peace, patience, kindness, goodness, faithfulness, gentleness, and self-control.

You will find that, in addition to teaching by example, you will actually grow with your disciple

Obviously, you cannot wait for inner perfection before you disciple another person. Be candid with him about your own weaknesses and struggles. Let him see you confess your shortcomings when you fail; invite him to pray with you through tough times. You will find that, in addition to teaching by example, you will actually grow *with* your disciple.

2. PRAY FOR HIM DAILY

Get the new Christian involved in a small-group Bible study.

Jesus prayed for His disciples and for all who would ultimately believe, including you and me (see John 17). The apostle Paul also prayed for all whom the Lord had placed in his charge. For example, in Ephesians 1:16–18 he wrote, "I pray for you constantly, asking God, the glorious Father of our Lord Jesus Christ, to give you spiritual wisdom and understanding, so that you might grow in your knowledge of God. I pray that your hearts will be flooded with light so that you can understand the wonderful future he has promised to those he called." Read that passage again, for it is an excellent recipe for the kind of prayer we should pray for friends who have recently found Jesus.

3. TEACH AND MODEL SPIRITUAL GROWTH

As you continue to meet with your new Christian friend, follow-up will mature into discipleship as you take him from "milk" to "solid food." Teaching the truths necessary for Christian growth involves a number of important topics (most of which are covered in "The Joy of Knowing God" series cited on page 107).

ASSURANCE OF SALVATION

Be sure he has assurance of his salvation, according to the promises (FACT) of God's Word. Revelation 3:20; Hebrews 13:5; and 1 John 5:11–13 are essential promises that every new

Christian should memorize. Review these passages with him several times during the first few weeks, repeating the questions: (1) "Where is Jesus Christ right now in relation to you? How do you know?" (see Revelation 3:20 and Hebrews 13:5); and (2) "When you die, what will happen to you?" (see 1 John 5:11–13). *The Joy of Finding Jesus* addresses this vital topic.

THE LORDSHIP OF CHRIST

Encourage him to make Christ the Lord of his life, according

❖

It is impossible to become a mature disciple without an understanding of God's Word.

to Romans 12:1–2; Galatians 2:20; and similar passages. People are so created that we do not find fulfillment until we have acknowledged our accountability to God and have obeyed His commands. Emphasize that there is no such thing as a joyful, fulfilled, *disobedient* Christian. Conversely, there are no truly *obedient* Christians who do not experience joy regardless of their circumstances.

Teach him by being an example, by instructing him in God's Word, and by introducing him to other godly men and women. Help him see the difference between the lifestyle of the nonbeliever, the worldly believer, and one who has made Christ the Lord of his or her life.

THE MINISTRY OF THE HOLY SPIRIT

Teach him how to walk in the control and power of the Holy Spirit. To emphasize Christian living without a proper understanding of the personal ministry of the Holy Spirit will only lead to frustration, legalism, and defeat.

The most liberating truth you can teach your disciple is

the concept of "Spiritual Breathing": how to "exhale" spiritually by confessing sin and how to "inhale" spiritually by appropriating the control and cleansing of God's Spirit by faith. *The Joy of Spirit-Filled Living* and *The Joy of Total Forgiveness* can be of significant help in understanding how to harness the power of the Holy Spirit in living the victorious Christian life.

THE IMPORTANCE OF GOD'S WORD

Help him understand the importance of reading the Word of God regularly and of studying it, memorizing it, and meditating on its truths daily. The Bible is God's holy, inspired Word to humankind. It is impossible to become a mature disciple without an understanding of God's Word. Help your disciple realize that every spiritual and practical problem he will ever encounter has an answer in the Word of God, directly or indirectly.

THE IMPORTANCE OF CHRISTIAN FELLOWSHIP

Teach him the importance of Christian fellowship, especially through the local church and through a small-group Bible study. Christians need each other for encouragement, caring, learning from one another, and accountability to each other. Encourage your disciple to be baptized and to join a caring, Bible-teaching fellowship of believers. Baptism is part of one's commitment to Christ that is often overlooked in the follow-up process. In the Great Commission, Jesus said, "As you go making disciples, baptize

> *Teach your friend that God longs to converse with him anytime, anywhere.*

them and teach them." It is important for believers to be baptized as an act of obedience and as public testimony of their commitment to Christ.

THE PRIVILEGE OF PRAYER

New life in Jesus Christ gives us direct access to the heavenly Father, 24/7! If we truly comprehended what an awesome honor this is, I believe we would spend far more time in prayer than we do. Teach your friend that God longs to converse with him anytime, anywhere—about anything! Assure him that God doesn't care how articulate our words may be—only that we maintain ongoing communion with Him. Consider using *The Joy of Active Prayer* when covering this important subject.

UNCONDITIONAL LOVE

Emphasize the importance of loving others unconditionally. Read the great passages in the Scriptures that emphasize love (especially 1 Corinthians 13), and ask God to demonstrate that quality in your own life as an example. As Jesus reminds us in John 13:35, "By this all men will know that you are my disciples, if you love one another" (NIV).

GOOD STEWARDSHIP

We must never forget that everything we have is a gift from God. Help your disciple understand the principle of honoring God in the way he uses his mind, body, and spirit as well as his time, talent, and treasure. Help him plan and use his time wisely; encourage him to develop his abilities and utilize them in the Lord's work; and help him learn to use his money wisely to lay up treasures in heaven. *The Joy of Dynamic Giving* can be of significant help for this subject.

How to Share Jesus

You shared Jesus with your friend and God changed his life; now imagine the joy he'll experience when he passes it on! It is not enough merely to explain methods, techniques, and strategies, nor is it enough to have him learn to use *The Four Spiritual Laws.* Just as one learns to pray by praying, so one learns to witness by witnessing. Earlier I recommended that each Christian develop a three-minute personal testimony; now is an excellent time to help your friend with this exercise. Walk him through the basic training I have provided in this book, and let him practice the gospel presentation with you; then once he has observed you in two or three sharing opportunities, ask him to handle the next one.

The Great Command

Finally, impart a vision for the fulfillment of the Great Commission of our Lord and Savior. For example, if your disciple is a student, plan together how he can help spread the gospel in classes, dorms, or other segments of the campus population. If your disciple is married, share how he and his spouse can win and disciple the couples in their neighborhood for Christ. If you are working with a businesswoman, show her how she can start Bible studies and evangelistic luncheons to help reach others in the business community.

These types of outreaches are being conducted successfully, every day, by Christians compelled by the love of Jesus Christ to share the greatest news ever announced. And while you impart a vision for your disciple's personal spheres of influence, help him understand the privilege and responsibility of helping reach the entire world as well (see Acts 1:8).

WHAT ABOUT DISCIPLING FAILURES?

Often I have shed tears of heartache and sorrow over men and women into whose lives I have poured much time and prayer, only to have them drift away to dishonor the Lord. Then God reminded me that they were His responsibility. He reminded me of how Christ's parable of the sower teaches that not all seed falls on good soil—some people fall away. While this can be disappointing, I have learned that I need to keep on trusting God and not be discouraged in my efforts to win and build men and women for Him. Just as successful witnessing is simply taking the initiative to share Christ in the power of the Holy Spirit and leaving the results to God, so:

> ## SUCCESSFUL FOLLOW-UP
> *Successful follow-up is simply taking the initiative to build disciples in the power of the Holy Spirit and leaving the results to God.*

Take follow-up and disciple building seriously—they go hand in glove with successful witnessing. Never forsake a witnessing opportunity just because you don't feel you would be able to provide follow-up. Modern communications provide myriad ways to stay in contact, and you can always network a new believer to a pastor or other Christian who will continue working with him.

Likewise, never forsake follow-up and disciple building with a new believer when the opportunity is there! Not only will you help a new Christian brother or sister become a mature, caring member of the body of Christ, but you will also experience the indescribable blessing of being God's chosen vessel in this rewarding calling.

God is an all-powerful, loving, wise, and compassionate heavenly Father. Nothing is too hard for Him. He is looking for true disciples—men and women willing to put their lives on the line for Him, willing to use their resources to win, build, train, and send others to help fulfill His Great Command. I challenge you to join me and millions of other Christians in taking the most joyful news ever announced to every person on earth—one soul at a time. God will richly bless you for your obedience. And you will experience the reality of our Lord's promise to reveal Himself to all who love and obey Him.

Readers' Guide

For Personal Reflection
or Group Discussion

Questions are an inevitable part of life. Proud parents ask their new baby, "Can you smile?" Later they ask, "Can you say 'Mama'?" "Can you walk to Daddy?" The early school years bring the inevitable, "What did you learn at school today?" Later school years introduce tougher questions, "If X equals 12 and Y equals –14, then …?" Adulthood adds a whole new set of questions. "Should I remain single or marry?" "How did things go at the office?" "Did you get a raise?" "Should we let Susie start dating?" "Which college is right for Kyle?" "How can we possibly afford to send our kids to college?"

This book raises questions too. The following study guide is designed to (1) maximize the subject material and (2) apply biblical truth to daily life. You won't be asked to solve any algebraic problems or recall dates associated with obscure events in history, so relax. Questions asking for objective information are based solely on the text. Most questions, however, prompt you to search inside your soul, examine the circumstances that surround your life, and decide how you can best use the truths communicated in the book.

Honest answers to real issues can strengthen your faith, draw you closer to the Lord, and lead you into fuller, richer, more joyful, and productive daily adventures. So confront each question head-on and expect the One who is the answer for all of life's questions and needs to accomplish great things in your life.

CHAPTER 1: THE SHY OVERACHIEVER

1. Why does it seem so hard to share our faith? What person or group do you find it most difficult to talk to about Christ? Why is it so difficult to talk to this person or group about Christ?

2. When Jesus commissioned His disciples to proclaim the gospel, were they different from us or quite similar to us? What conclusion about sharing our faith can you draw from this comparison?

3. How would you characterize Bill Bright's landlords' efforts to evangelize him? What do you learn from their efforts?

4. What impressed you most as you read Bill Bright's conversion story?

5. How would you define "happiness"? How can a person find true happiness?

CHAPTER 2: TELLING MY FATHER ABOUT JESUS

1. Do you think some fear of sharing your faith can be a good thing? Why or why not?

2. Why should Christians maintain a positive attitude about sharing their faith?

3. Why do you agree or disagree that many people are thirsting for the knowledge of salvation?

4. Why is a believer's personal story of coming to Christ so powerful?

5. If a loved one told you he or she was leading a morally upright life and therefore didn't need to make a personal commitment to Christ, how would you respond?

CHAPTER 3: WHY SHARING JESUS MAKES SENSE

1. Why does it make sense to share Jesus with others?

2. Does a Christian need the gift of evangelism in order to share Jesus? Why or why not?

3. What evidence do you see in society that people want to feel loved?

4. What are a few popular philosophies that fail to satisfy the heart?

5. What does Dr. Bright cite as the best way to approach sharing Jesus with others? How might his advice improve or even revolutionize your approach to sharing Jesus?

CHAPTER 4: WHY SOME CHRISTIANS HESITATE

1. What excuses have you heard Christians offer to avoid sharing their faith?

2. How would you answer someone who says you should never discuss religion and politics?

3. How can Christians maintain ardent love for Jesus Christ?

4. How can a lethargic Christian rekindle his or her first love?

5. Which of the Devil's lines trouble you most? How will you ignore those lines and become a confident witness?

CHAPTER 5: CONQUERING THE FEAR OF FAILURE

1. Why does rejection hurt so much?

2. Whose conversion to Christ has made you realize that even an unlikely candidate for salvation can believe in Christ?

3. What role does prayer play in bringing a person to faith in Christ?'

4. Should Christians witness to people for whom they have not prayed? Why or why not?

5. How will your prayers be different as a result of reading chapter 5 of this book?

CHAPTER 6: GUIDING A CONVERSATION TOWARD JESUS

1. How might a Christian guide each of the following conversations toward Jesus. a conversation about the weather, a conversation about world news, a conversation about how quickly time passes?

2. What four directed questions does the author suggest for transitioning a conversation to the gospel?

3. What is the proper motivation for sharing the gospel? Is it possible to love sharing the gospel more than loving lost people? Why or why not?

4. Have you ever been sidetracked from sharing the gospel? What sidetracked you? What was the outcome? What did you learn from that experience?

5. What simple (but profound) truths should you share every time you witness?

CHAPTER 7: SHARING JESUS

1. What are *The Four Spiritual Laws?*

2. What benefits does Dr. Bright associate with the consistent presentation of *The Four Spiritual Laws?*

3. How does familiarity with *The Four Spiritual Laws* build confidence for witnessing?

4. What statement might a Christian use as he or she introduces *The Four Spiritual Laws?*

5. How would you assure a new believer that salvation is forever?

CHAPTER 8: HANDLING OBJECTIONS, HOSTILITY, QUESTIONS, AND RESISTANCE

1. What excuses do people sometimes give for resisting the gospel? How should Christians counter these excuses?

2. What common misconceptions of Christianity create ill will toward those who try to share their faith?

3. Must a person denounce evolution in order to become a Christian? Why or why not?

4. How would you describe the partnership that exists between God and the Christian in one-on-one evangelism?

5. What does Dr. Bright describe as the "30-Day Experiment"? Which of your friends or associates might be prime candidates for this experiment?

CHAPTER 9: LIVE IT!

1. Do you think most recent converts are receiving appropriate follow-up? How might Christians provide better nurturing of new believers?

2. How might a Christian nurture a new believer who lives in a distant place?

3. What urgent questions did you want answered when you were a new Christian? Do you agree that most new Christians entertain the same questions? If so, what are the satisfactory answers?

4. What five facts does the author suggest sharing with a new Christian?

5. How does Christian fellowship contribute to spiritual growth? What opportunities for Christian fellowship would you recommend?

Appendix A

The Letter

Dear Dr. Van Dusen:

Cordial greetings from sunny California! Thank you for your recent letter requesting additional information. The warm expression of your desire to know more about Jesus Christ encourages me to explain briefly the basic facts concerning the Christian life.

First, I would like to have you think of the Christian life as a great adventure, for Jesus said, "I am come that they might have life, and that they might have it more abundantly" (John 10:10 KJV).

Second, I want you to know that God loves us and has a wonderful, exciting plan for every life. We are not creatures of chance, brought into the world for a meaningless, miserable existence; rather, we are children of destiny, created for lives of purpose and joyful service to God and our fellow man. Any student knows that there are definite laws in the physical realm that are inviolate; just so, there are definite spiritual laws that govern our spiritual lives.

Since man is the highest known form of life, and since there is a purpose for everything else, does it not make sense that there is a plan for us? If God created us for a purpose, does it not logically follow that that purpose somehow, somewhere, has been revealed? Would this One who created us then leave us to shift for ourselves? All evidence would demonstrate the contrary.

How, then, can man know God's plan?

There are many religions, and most of them have their "sacred writings." Yet, when these are studied in an objective manner, it soon becomes evident that the Old and New Testaments of the Bible differ vastly from the others. Though there is much good in the writings of these various religions, it quickly becomes obvious that they in no way compare with the sacred Scriptures upon which Christianity is based.

While studying under some of the world's greatest scholars in two of our country's leading seminaries, it was proven conclusively to me that, in a unique and special way, God has spoken to men through the writings of the Bible.

Every man is seeking happiness, but the Bible says that true happiness can be found only through God's way. Let me explain simply what this way is. The Bible says that God is holy and man is sinful. There is a great chasm between them. Man is continually trying to find God (see diagram 1). From the most ignorant savage to the most brilliant professor on the university campus, man is trying to find God and the abundant life through his own efforts. Through the various philosophies and religions of history, man has tried to cross this chasm to find God and a life of purpose and happiness.

Man can no more bridge this chasm than he can jump across the Grand Canyon flat-footed, or climb to heaven on a six-foot ladder. The Bible explains that this is impossible because God is holy and righteous, and man is sinful. Man was created to have fellowship with God, but because of his own stubborn self-will and disobedience, man chose to go his own independent way—and fellowship was broken. That is what the Bible calls sin.

Pull the plug of a floor lamp from its wall socket, and contact with the electrical current is broken and the light goes out. This is comparable to what happens to man when fellowship with God is broken. The Bible says, "All have sinned, and come short of the glory of God" (Romans 3:23 KJV) and "The wages of sin is death; but the gift of God is eternal life through Jesus Christ our Lord" (Romans 6:23 KJV).

I am not saying that sin is a matter of getting drunk, committing murder, being immoral, etc. These are only the *result* of sin. What, then, are symptoms of a life separated from God? In addition to some of the grosser sins, they are, for some people: worry, irritability, lack of purpose in life, no goal, no power, no real interest in living, utter boredom, inferiority complex, frustration, desire to escape reality, and fear of death. These and many others are evidence that man is cut off from the only One who can give him the power to live the abundant life.

St. Augustine, one of the greatest philosophers and theologians of all time, said, "Thou hast made us for Thyself, O God, and our hearts are restless until they find their rest in Thee."

Pascal, the great physicist and philosopher, described the longing in the human heart this way: "There is a God-shaped vacuum in the heart of each man, which cannot be satisfied by any created thing but only by God, the Creator, made known through Jesus Christ."

Now if God has a plan for us, a plan that includes a full and abundant life, and all of man's efforts to find God are futile, then we must turn to the Bible to discover God's way.

The Bible tells us, "God so loved the world that he gave his only Son, so that everyone who believes in him will not perish but have eternal life" (John 3:16). In other words, this great chasm between

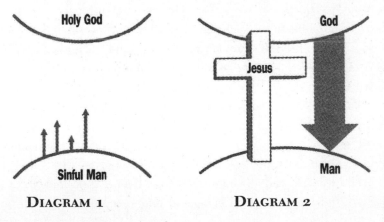

DIAGRAM 1   DIAGRAM 2

God and man cannot be bridged by man's effort, but only by God's effort through His Son, Jesus Christ.

Let me call your attention to the fact that we cannot know God through good works. "God saved you by his special favor when you believed. And you can't take credit for this; it is a gift from God. Salvation is not a reward for the good things we have done, so none of us can boast about it" (Ephesians 2:8–9). Good works will follow an acceptance of God's gift, as an expression of our gratitude.

Religion and philosophy have been defined as man's best attempts to reach God. Christianity is God's perfect plan to reach man.

W ho is this person Jesus Christ, that He, more than anyone who has ever lived, has the power to bridge this chasm between a holy God and sinful man? (See diagram 2.) Jesus of Nazareth was conceived by the Holy Spirit and born of the Virgin Mary two thousand years ago. Hundreds of years before, great prophets of Israel foretold His coming. The Old Testament, which was written by many individuals over a period of fifteen hundred years, contains more than three hundred references to His coming. At the age of thirty, He began His public ministry. Space will not allow for details except to say that, in the three years following, He gave man the formula for a full and abundant life, and for eternal life to come.

The life Jesus led, the miracles He performed, the words He spoke, His death on the cross, His resurrection, His ascent to heaven, all point to the fact that He was not a mere man, but more than man. He himself claimed to be God. "I and my Father are one" (John 10:30 KJV); and "He that hath seen me hath seen the Father" (John 14:9 KJV).

The late Arnold Toynbee, one of the most eminent historians of our century, has given more space to Jesus of Nazareth than to any other six great men who have ever lived, including Muhammad, Buddha, Caesar, Napoleon, and George Washington.

The Encyclopædia Britannica devotes twenty thousand words to Jesus. Thinking men of all lands and religions who investigate the evidence will agree that Jesus is the greatest personality the world has ever known.

It is important to consider that Jesus Christ claimed to be God. He claimed to be the author of a new way of life. Historically, we know that wherever His message has gone, new life, new hope, and new purpose for living have resulted. Either Jesus of Nazareth was who He claimed to be—the Son of God, the Savior of mankind— or He was the greatest impostor the world has ever known. If His claims were false, more good has resulted from a lie than has ever been accomplished by the truth. Does it not make sense that this person (whom most people knowing the facts consider the greatest teacher, the greatest example, the greatest leader the world has ever known) would be, as He himself claimed to be and as the Bible tells us that He is, the one person who could bridge the chasm between God and man?

You will remember Romans 6.23, to which I referred: "For the wages of sin is death; but the gift of God is eternal life through Jesus Christ our Lord" (KJV). As you study the religions and philosophies of the world, you will find no provision for man's sin apart from the cross of Jesus Christ. The Bible says that without the shedding of blood there is no remission or forgiveness of sin (see Hebrews 9:22). In Acts 4:12 we are told: "There is salvation in no one else! There is no other name in all of heaven for people to call on to save them." Jesus himself said, "I am the way, the truth, and the life. No one can come to the Father except through me" (John 14:6).

Let me show you what Jesus said to a man who came to Him for counsel. Nicodemus was a Pharisee, a ruler of the Jews, one of the great religious leaders of his day. So far as the law was concerned, he was above reproach. He was moral and ethical. He was so eager to please God that he prayed seven times a day. He went to the synagogue to worship God three times a day. Yet he saw in the life of Jesus something that he had never experienced himself; there was a different quality of life altogether.

Nicodemus approached Jesus saying, "'Teacher, we all know that

God has sent you to teach us. Your miraculous signs are proof enough that God is with you.'

"Jesus replied, 'I assure you, unless you are born again, you can never see the Kingdom of God.'

"'What do you mean?' exclaimed Nicodemus. 'How can an old man go back into his mother's womb and be born again?'

"Jesus replied, 'The truth is, no one can enter the Kingdom of God without being born of water and the Spirit. Humans can reproduce only human life, but the Holy Spirit gives new life from heaven. So don't be surprised at my statement that you must be born again'" (John 3:2–7).

What is this new birth? Consider, for example, a caterpillar crawling in the dust—an ugly, hairy worm. One day this worm weaves about its body a cocoon. From this cocoon there emerges a beautiful butterfly. We do not understand fully what has taken place. We realize only that where once an ugly worm crawled in the dust, now a beautiful butterfly soars in the skies. So it is in the lives of Christians. Where once we lived on the lowest level as sinful, egocentric individuals, we now dwell on the highest plane, experiencing full and abundant lives as children of God.

An individual becomes a Christian through a spiritual rebirth. In other words, God is spirit, and we cannot communicate with Him until we become spiritual creatures. (This is what takes place when Jesus comes to live in our lives.) Without His indwelling presence, we cannot communicate with God; we know nothing of His plan for our lives; the Word of God is a dull, uninteresting book. However, when Jesus comes into our lives and we become Spirit controlled, we love to be with Christians, we love to read the Word of God, and we want our lives to count for Him. Just suppose, for the sake of illustration, that we are sitting in a room and we know that there are a number of television programs available to us. We are looking and listening, yet we cannot see the images or hear the voices. What is needed? An instrument—a television set. The moment we move a television set into the room and turn it on, we can hear a voice and see an image. So it is when

Christ comes into our lives. He is our divine instrument, tuning us in to God, making known God's will and love for our lives.

Basically, the only thing that separates an individual from God—and thus from His love and forgiveness—is his own self-will. (Please do not think me presumptuous. I do not wish to embarrass you by encouraging you to do anything that you are reluctant to do. However, because you expressed such genuine interest in knowing more about these matters when we talked face-to-face, I am taking the liberty, as one who sincerely cares, by encouraging you to enter into this relationship with Christ today!)

Well do I remember that night several years ago when, alone in my room, I knelt to surrender my will to the will of Christ. While in prayer, I invited Him to enter the "door" of my life, forgive my sin, and take His rightful place on the throne. I must confess that there was no great emotional response, as some have had—actually none at all—but, true to His promise, Christ came in. And gradually, like the blooming of a lovely rose, the beauty and fragrance of His presence became real to me. Though in my spiritual ignorance as a nonbeliever I had considered myself to be perfectly happy and fulfilled with life, He gave me a new and genuine quality of life altogether—a promise of abundant life fulfilled in ways too numerous to mention.

God loves you so much that He gave His only Son to die on the cross for your sins; and Jesus Christ, the Son of God, loved you enough to die on the cross for you. Here He is, the greatest leader, the greatest teacher, the greatest example the world has ever known. But more than this, He is the Son of God, the Savior. Can you think of anyone whom you would rather follow?

Perhaps you are thinking, *Suppose I invite Christ into my life and nothing happens? Maybe the Lord will not hear me.* May I assure you that you can trust Christ. He promised to come in. He does not lie. A chemist going into a laboratory to work on an experiment knows that, by following the Table of Chemical Valence, he will get the desired results. The mathematician knows that the multiplication table is tried and dependable, and that the law of gravity is inviolate. Just so, the laws of the spiritual realm are definite and true, and when God, who created all things and established the laws that govern all things, says that He will enter and change your life, you may accept this promise without question.

Jesus said, "'Look! Here I stand at the door and knock. If you hear me calling and open the door, I will come in, and we will share a meal as friends'" (Revelation 3:20). He has come to forgive your sins. He has come to bring peace and purpose to your life: "I am come that they might have life, and they might have it more abundantly" (John 10:10 KJV).

Our lives are filled with many activities such as business, travel, finances, social life, and home life, often with no real purpose or meaning. Jesus knocks at the heart's door, seeking entrance. He will not force himself. Jesus wants to come into your life and make harmony out of discord—to create meaning and purpose where now there is something lacking. He wants to forgive your sin and bridge the gulf between you and God. He does not want to enter your life as a guest, but He wants to control your life as Lord and Master.

Imagine a "throne" in each heart. All of these years, your ego has been on the throne. Jesus Christ waits for you to invite Him to be on the throne:

Self-Directed Life
S – Self is on the throne
† – Christ is outside the life
● – Interests are directed by self, often resulting in discord and frustration

†

Christ-Directed Life
† – Christ is in the life and on the throne
S – Self is yielding to Christ
● – Interests are directed by Christ, resulting in harmony with God's plan

When Christ becomes Lord of your life, He becomes Lord of every activity. As the simple diagram above illustrates, this makes for a harmonious life. Is it not better to be controlled by the infinite, loving God who created you and suffered for you than to continue under the control of finite self? "Therefore if any man be in Christ, he is a new creature: old things are passed away; behold, all things are become new" (2 Corinthians 5:17 KJV).

Will you not sincerely invite the Lord Jesus into your heart and surrender your will completely to Him, right now? We can talk with God through prayer. Why not find a quiet place where you can kneel or bow reverently in God's presence and ask Christ to come into your heart? In your prayer, you can say something like this:

> *"Lord Jesus, I need You. Thank You for dying on the cross for my sins. I open the door of my life and receive You as my Savior and Lord. Thank You for forgiving my sins and giving me eternal life. Take control of the throne of my life. Make me the kind of person You want me to be."*

To invite Christ into your life is absolutely the most important decision you will ever make; and when you do so, several wonderful things will happen:

1. Christ will actually come to live in your heart.
2. Your sins will be forgiven.
3. You will truly become a child of God.
4. You are assured of heaven.
5. Your life becomes a great adventure, as God reveals His plan and purpose and as you continue to live in faith and obedience.

Did you ask Christ into your heart? Were you sincere? Where is He right now? In the event that you are disappointed because there may have been no great emotional experience—though some may indeed know this immediate joy—I want to remind you again that a Christian must place his faith in the Word of God, not in feelings; for emotions come and go, but the Word of God is trustworthy and true. Christ promised to enter when you opened the door. He does not lie. (Meditate again on the truth of Revelation 3:20; John 1:12; 1 John 5:11–13; 2 Corinthians 5:17.) Take time right now to thank God for what has happened to you as you have prayed.

Since you have never been satisfied with mediocrity in your business, you will certainly not want to be an ordinary Christian. It costs us nothing to become Christians, although it cost God His own dear Son to give us this privilege. But it will cost us both time and effort to be the kind of Christian God would have us be. For obvious reasons, a Christian should be a better businessperson, parent, spouse, student, or whatever role he or she fulfills.

Here is a suggestion that will enable you to grow quickly in the Christian life, illustrated by a simple little word "GROWTH":

G   Go to God in prayer daily.

R   Read God's Word daily, beginning with the gospel of John.

O   Obey God, moment by moment.

W   Witness for Christ by your life and words.

T   Trust God for every detail of your life.

H   Holy Spirit—allow Him to control and empower your daily life and actions (Galatians 5:16–17; Acts 1:8).

In Hebrews 10:25, we are admonished to forsake not "the assembling of ourselves together" (KJV). Several logs burn brightly together; put one aside on the cold hearth and the fire goes out. So it is with you and your relationship with other Christians. If you do not belong to a church, do not wait to be invited. Take the initiative; call the pastor of a nearby church where Christ is honored and the Bible is preached. Make plans to start next Sunday and to attend each week.

Be assured of my love and prayers as you make this all-important decision. We shall be looking forward to hearing from you soon.

Sincerely yours,
WILLIAM R. BRIGHT

Appendix B

God's Word on Sharing Jesus

Following are selected Scripture references that were presented throughout the text of this book. We encourage you to sit down with your Bible and review these verses in their context, prayerfully reflecting upon what God's Word tells you about sharing Jesus. You may wish to focus especially on the references listed for chapter 7, "Sharing Jesus," as they are at the core of the gospel message.

CHAPTER 1

John 3:16
Matthew 28:19
Revelation 3:20

CHAPTER 2

Matthew 4:19
Mark 16:15–16
Ephesians 2:8–9

CHAPTER 3

John 14:6

CHAPTER 4

1 John 1:9
Ephesians 6:12
Colossians 1:13
Matthew 9:37

CHAPTER 5

Matthew 13:3–8
Matthew 13:23
2 Peter 3:9

CHAPTER 7

John 10:10
Romans 3:23
Romans 6:23
Romans 5:8
1 Corinthians
15:3–6
John 1:12
John 3:1–8
1 John 5:11–13
John 14:21

Hebrews 13:5

Colossians 1:27

Colossians 1:14

John 5:24

2 Corinthians 5:17

1 Thessalonians
   5:18

Galatians 3:11

John 15:7

Acts 17:11

John 15:8

1 Peter 5:7

Galatians 5:16–17

Acts 1:8

Hebrews 10:25

CHAPTER 9

Colossians 1:28

John 17

Ephesians 1:16–18

Romans 12:1–2

Galatians 2:20

1 Corinthians 13

John 13:35

About the Author

DR. BILL BRIGHT, fueled by his passion to share the love and claims of Jesus Christ with "every living person on earth," was the founder and president of Campus Crusade for Christ. The world's largest Christian ministry, Campus Crusade serves people in 191 countries through a staff of 26,000 full-time employees and more than 225,000 trained volunteers working in some sixty targeted ministries and projects that range from military ministry to inner-city ministry.

Bill Bright was so motivated by what is known as the Great Commission, Christ's command to carry the gospel throughout the world, that in 1956 he wrote a booklet titled *The Four Spiritual Laws*, which has been printed in 200 languages and distributed to more than 2.5 billion people. Other books Bright authored include *Discover the Book God Wrote, God: Discover His Character, Come Help Change Our World, The Holy Spirit: The Key to Supernatural Living, Life Without Equal, Witnessing Without Fear, Coming Revival, Journey Home,* and *Red Sky in the Morning.*

In 1979 Bright commissioned the *JESUS* film, a feature-length dramatization of the life of Christ. To date, the film has been viewed by more than 5.7 billion people in 191 countries and has become the most widely viewed and translated film in history.

Dr. Bright died in July 2003 before the final editing of this book. But he prayed that it would leave a legacy of his love for Jesus and the power of the Holy Spirit to change lives. He is survived by his wife, Vonette; their sons and daughters-in-law; and four grandchildren.

THE LIFETIME TEACHINGS OF

Written by one of Christianity's most respected and beloved teachers, this series is a must for every believer's library. Each of the books in the series focuses on a vital aspect of a meaningful life of faith: trusting God, accepting Christ, living a spirit-filled life, intimacy with God, forgiveness, prayer, obedience, supernatural thinking, giving, and sharing Christ with others.

Dr. Bill Bright was the founder of Campus Crusade for Christ Intl., the world's largest Christian ministry. He commissioned the JESUS film, a documentary on the life of Christ that has been translated into more than 800 languages.

EACH BOOK INCLUDES A CELEBRITY-READ ABRIDGED AUDIO CD!

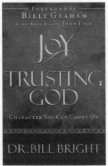
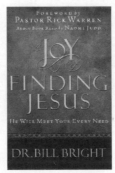

Joy of Trusting God
Foreword by Billy Graham
Audio by John Tesh
0-78144-246-X

Joy of Finding Jesus
Foreword by Pastor
Rick Warren
Audio by Naomi Judd
0-78144-247-8

Joy of Spirit-Filled Living
Foreword by Kay Arthur
Audio by Ricky Skaggs
0-78144-248-6

DR. BILL BRIGHT

FOUNDER OF CAMPUS CRUSADE FOR CHRIST

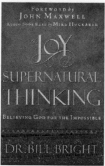

Joy of Supernatural Thinking
Foreword by John Maxwell
Audio by Gov. Mike Huckabee
0-78144-253-2

Joy of Dynamic Giving
Foreword by Charles Stanley
Audio by John Schneider
0-78144-254-0

Joy of Sharing Jesus
Foreword by Pat Robertson
Audio by Kathie Lee Gifford
0-78144-255-9

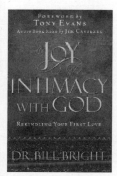

Joy of Intimacy with God
Foreword by Tony Evans
Audio by Amy Grant
0-78144-249-4

Joy of Total Forgiveness
Foreword by Gary Smalley
Audio by Janine Turner
0-78144-250-8

Joy of Active Prayer
Foreword by Max Lucado
Audio by Joni Earekcson Tada
0-78144-251-6

Joy of Faithful Obedience
Foreword by Tim LaHaye
Audio by Kirk Franklin
0-78144-252-4

Collect all 10 of These Foundational Works!

The Word at Work Around the World

A vital part of Cook Communications Ministries is our international outreach, Cook Communications Ministries International (CCMI). Your purchase of this book, and of other books and Christian-growth products from Cook, enables CCMI to provide Bibles and Christian literature to people in more than 150 languages in 65 countries.

Cook Communications Ministries is a not-for-profit, self-supporting organization. Revenues from sales of our books, Bible curricula, and other church and home products not only fund our U.S. ministry, but also fund our CCMI ministry around the world. One hundred percent of donations to CCMI go to our international literature programs.

CCMI reaches out internationally in three ways:

· Our premier International Christian Publishing Institute (ICPI) trains leaders from nationally led publishing houses around the world.

· We provide literature for pastors, evangelists, and Christian workers in their national language.

· We reach people at risk—refugees, AIDS victims, street children, and famine victims—with God's Word.

Word Power, God's Power

Faith Kidz, RiverOak, Honor, Life Journey, Victor, NexGen — every time you purchase a book produced by Cook Communications Ministries, you not only meet a vital personal need in your life or in the life of someone you love, but you're also a part of ministering to José in Colombia, Humberto in Chile, Gousa in India, or Lidiane in Brazil. You help make it possible for a pastor in China, a child in Peru, or a mother in West Africa to enjoy a life-changing book. And because you helped, children and adults around the world are learning God's Word and walking in his ways.

Thank you for your partnership in helping to disciple the world. May God bless you with the power of his Word in your life.

For more information about our international ministries, visit www.ccmi.org.

Additional copies of
THE JOY OF SHARING JESUS
and other titles in "The Joy of Knowing God" series
are available wherever good books are sold.

✠ ✠ ✠

If you have enjoyed this book,
or if it has had an impact on your life,
we would like to hear from you.

Please contact us at:

VICTOR BOOKS
Cook Communications Ministries, Dept. 201
4050 Lee Vance View
Colorado Springs, CO 80918

Or at our Web site: www.cookministries.com

Victor®
The Bible Teacher's Teacher